French Chic

French

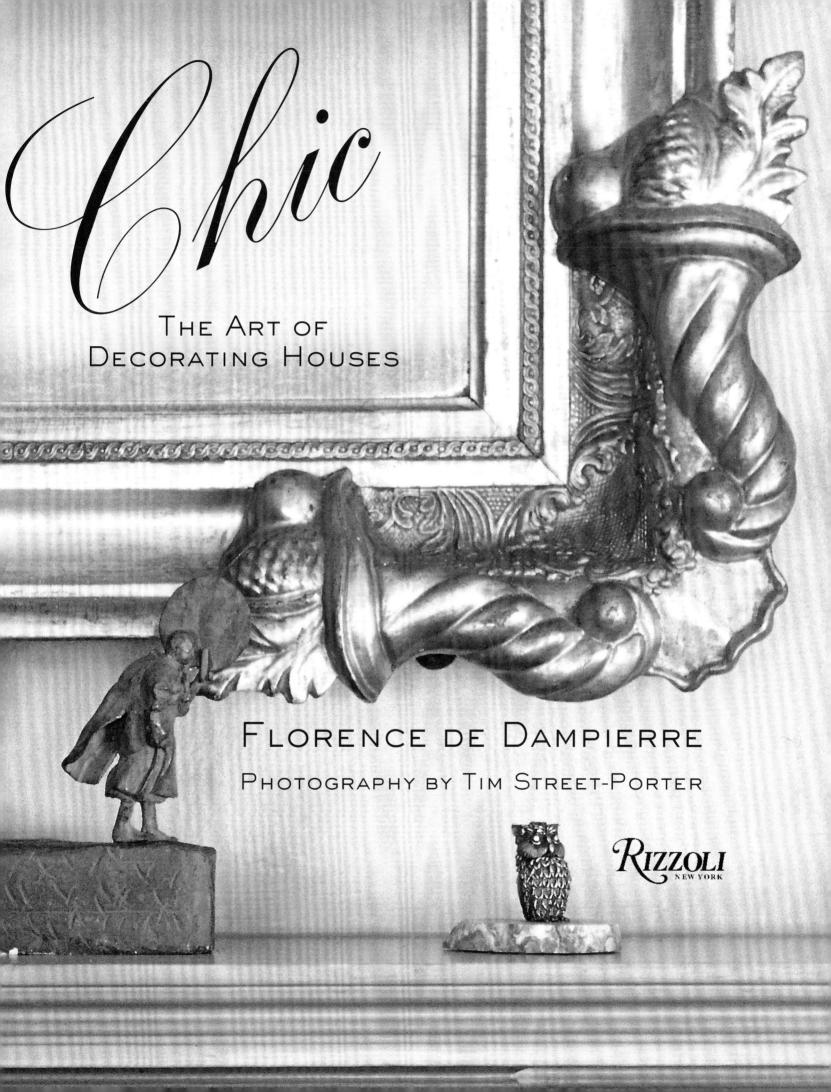

Chic

THE ART OF DECORATING HOUSES

FLORENCE DE DAMPIERRE

PHOTOGRAPHY BY TIM STREET-PORTER

RIZZOLI
NEW YORK

PAGE 2–3: The bottom of an American gilded mirror in the library.
PAGE 6: Ma Maison, a view from the back of the house.

First published in the United States of America in 2008
by Rizzoli International Publications, Inc.
300 Park Avenue South
New York, New York 10010
www.rizzoliusa.com

2008 2009 2010 2011 / 10 9 8 7 6 5 4 3 2 1

Printed in China

ISBN-13: 978-0-8478-3059-6

Library of Congress Catalog Control Number: 2008928756

Project Editor: Sandra Gilbert

Designers: Joel Avirom, Jason Snyder, and Meghan Day Healey

Production: Kaija Markoe

ACKNOWLEDGMENTS

French Chic is a tribute to my parents, family, and friends in France who have influenced my life and contributed to the creation of wonderful memories. I thank you from the bottom of my heart.

This opus has been a pleasurable project and I hope that the fun we had in creating it comes through. The exquisite photographs are the work of Tim Street-Porter—I could not thank him enough. Tim has the rare quality of infusing his beautiful photography with charm. It is a rare pleasure to work with such a talented, sweet, and fun person. We enjoyed immensely our lunches spent eating props and planning the next shots! We have had a lovely time of it.

This book is also a tribute to my friends with whom I have shared countless happy moments. They have always been supportive in one way or another. I wish to thank Dana and Edwin Schulman, Joseph Montebello, Ron Leal, Peggy Tagliarino, Tom Fallon, Dale Ryan, Sylvia Charvillat, Nabil Nahas, John and Kate Fahey, Bobby Smith, Christine McCarty, Terry Campion, Ann Rapp, Masha Nudell, Stephen McGruder, Susan and Jay Swatzburg, and Wolfram Koppe, among many others. A very special nod to Annie Kelly, who has been the best technical support and more! My deepest gratitude goes to my friends Angeline Goreau, who has always helped and guided me, and Fran Kiernan for her invaluable editing advice. I also wish to thank my friend and co-worker Joszef Cziotka—as well as his crew, Tomas and Gabor—who is personally responsible for building many of the spaces we can admire in this book. Our long collaboration has been most enjoyable.

Many thanks also to the diligent work of my delightful editor, Sandy Gilbert. She managed to make the most grueling part of the book fun! This is quite a compliment. It is a pleasure to be back at Rizzoli; my deepest thanks go to Charles Miers and the whole team. I wish to especially thank Joel Avirom, Jason Snyder, and Meghan Day Healey for their warm and inspiring graphic design. It is the final piece of the puzzle and a lovely one.

Finally, I thank my husband Sean for his constant support, and my children Aymar, Cameron, and Valentina who have been most helpful and are excited to see this new project come to fruition. It is part of their life too, after all.

Merci.

Contents

INTRODUCTION

Ma Maison

La personalité des gens comme les immeubles ont des façades differentes,

certaines plaisantes, d'autre pas.

(Like buildings, people's personalities have various facades—

some pleasant to view, some not.)

—François de La Rochefoucauld (1613–80)

SEVERAL YEARS AGO, a year or so after the birth of my daughter, my husband and I decided to look for a house in Litchfield, Connecticut, instead of trying to expand the place we were living in at the time. A good friend of ours, John, a real-estate agent in this rural area, suggested that we go and have a look at several houses for starters, to educate ourselves. Excited by the thought of checking out the way people live, as I am a true *voyeur*, I soldiered right on into our little sightseeing expedition.

The first house we visited was near the center of this picturesque New England town, on North Street. Sinclair Lewis is credited with saying: *The only street in Litchfield that is more beautiful than South Street is North Street.* Few would argue the point. This is a town that has always had a special appeal for my husband and me. One of the main reasons is because it is a real place with a town green surrounded by several shops, restaurants (including a very good one), and churches. Litchfield also has a rich history, which in my book is always a plus. Founded in 1721, Litchfield is home to the first law school in America, as well as the first "female

OPPOSITE: French bistro chairs and tables around the pool are perfect surfaces to hold refreshing glasses of lemonade for the thirsty swimmer and are a good visual addition to an old American Colonial house.

RIGHT: An old postcard of North Street in Litchfield, Connecticut, shows a view from the green.

NORTH STREET - LITCHFIELD, CONN.

9

ABOVE AND OPPOSITE: *Bonjour!* Welcome. Here I am standing in front of the door of Ma Maison, wearing green, one of my favorite colors. The Federal door, painted a wonderful lime green, is a dead giveaway and makes the relatively traditional Colonial-style building more whimsical.

academy," established by Sally Pierce. In 1753, Oliver Wolcott, one of the signers of the Declaration of Independence, built a house, which is still standing, where he entertained General George Washington and his friend, the Marquis de Lafayette (a French connection).

Following the Revolutionary War, Litchfield was one of the most important cultural centers in America. Of the 1,200 residents listed in early records, many were highly educated and held positions of power. In fact, seventeen were college graduates, seven were captains in the Continental Army, four became generals, four were elected to Congress, and two were nominated chief justices. Litchfield can also boast that two of the state's governors came from her town. Quite a group! Not to mention, it was also home to Harriet Beecher Stowe, the author of *Uncle Tom's Cabin*.

John and I walked into the house. Despite the run-down quality of the place, its charm and excellent bones seduced me immediately. It's a bit unbelievable that the first thing we looked at seemed to fit all our requirements to a T. We checked the house from top to bottom, from the attic to the wine cellar. On one wall of the wine cellar I noticed very distinctive old-style French handwriting, reminiscent of my grandmother's script. The bottles from the house's wine collection—Mouton-Rothschild, Cheval-Blanc, Château-Eyquem, and assorted Saint-Emilions—had been recorded there. Unfortunately no bottles were lying around, but what a strange coincidence for me, being a Frenchwoman! In fact, it was rumored that one of the previous owners was none other than a French countess—hence, the fine wine collection and the familiar French handwriting.

The house was a little bit like the *château de la belle au bois dormants*; it needed to be awakened from a long, long sleep. Although the house needed much work, we were immediately sold on it and made the purchase. We then proceeded to lovingly restore our new home back to its original beauty, starting with such non-sexy essentials as roofing, electrical wiring, and plumbing. Soon, but not soon enough—as anyone involved with major renovations knows—structural work graduated to more rewarding aspects, such as the construction of French doors, floors, and moldings, as well as the selection of the color palettes. The place slowly came back to life; its reworked floor plan was more fitting for today's family life, with the incessant movements of dogs and children as well as the coming and going of friends of all ages.

The house, despite its mix of Colonial and Federal styles, feels very French, but not in a predictable way. Do not expect a plethora of over-gilded Louis-Louis type furniture or Provençal fruitwood chairs. French taste is much more than these narrow stereotypes. In the words of Edith Wharton, *French taste? It's the way the women put on their hats, and the upholsterers drape their curtains.* Now please follow me on a historical journey of French decoration and a private tour of my house. You will then understand what French chic is all about. *C'est la vie!*

OPPOSITE: Plants, greenery, and a picket fence add a homey touch to the inside.

ABOVE: This is where all my ideas come from—my office, which boasts a great view of the garden.

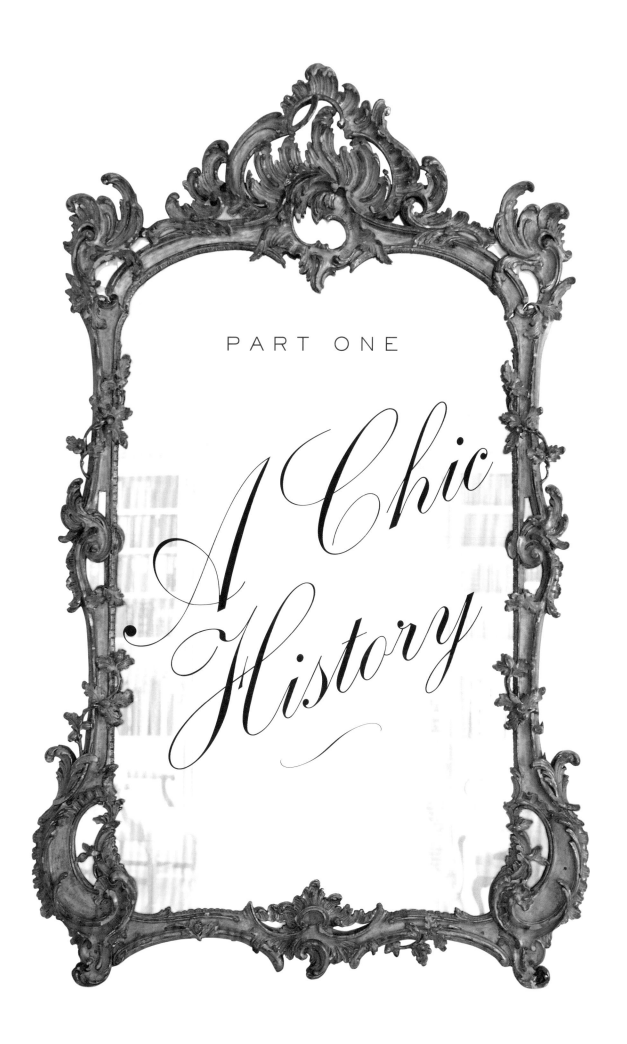

PART ONE

A Chic History

The Historical Tradition

French taste? Why, of course—everybody knows all about that! It's the way the women put on their hats, and the upholsterers drape their curtains.

—Edith Wharton (1862–1937),
French Ways and Their Meaning, 1919

TODAY WE LIVE IN A SOCIETY in which more and more people take an active interest in home design. As the years go by, a larger segment of the population spends time and money on it. This is a multi-billion dollar industry for people trying to create the ideal home.

What is the ideal home? Every civilization before ours had specific ideas about decoration based on their traditions and way of life. Our notion of the ideal home has evolved through time. Knowing about the past and changing fashions is a necessity in order to master the future. The more you know, the more easily you can make clever choices and decisions that are appropriate for you. In a word, the path to happiness in home design is through knowledge. It is a small price to pay in order to create a perfect home.

Since the beginning of time, the desire to create for oneself or one's family a nest of comfort has been apparent. The wall decorations in the Grottes de Lascaux during the Paleolithic Age, around 14,000 B.C., speak volumes about the human cocooning instinct. They show that humans from very early on tried through painting and decoration to personalize their surroundings, even when it was just a cave.

The Egyptians shared similar beliefs. Their lavishly decorated pyramids were supposed to make the afterlife of their ruler as comfortable and as close to their earthly life as possible. Beautiful furniture inlaid with precious stones, ivory, or rare woods was set on fur rugs in carefully decorated rooms.

For the Greeks, beauty was harmony, balance, and proportion as their proud buildings, which are still standing, keep reminding us. Remember the glorious Parthenon or the Temple of Poseidon at Paestum—their classic simplicity is haunting. The classical tradition continued with Rome and its awe-inspiring buildings such as the Colosseum or the Trojan Arch, alongside warm, colorful, and sophisticated decorations, paintings, or mosaics, as the ruins of Pompeii and Herculaneum have revealed.

PAGE 14: A *sultane,* signed Jean Avisse. Musée Nissan de Camondo, Paris. Photo: Antoine Bootz.

OPPOSITE: Design for a candelabra (detail) by Aimé Chenavard (1798–1838). This bejeweled gold candelabra features putti and tasseled embellishments. The Metropolitan Museum of Art, The Elisha Whittelsey Fund, 1958.

Beginning with antiquity, architecture, design, and decoration have been walking hand in hand, as they should, in the creation of successful buildings. This is exactly what happened in France in the seventeenth century, for the first time in Europe. A truly national style of interior decoration was created on a grand scale at Vaux-le-Vicomte, which was built with unusual rapidity between 1657 and 1661, to the design of the famous architect Louis Le Vau (1612–70), for Nicolas Fouquet, Louis XIV's enormously wealthy Surintendant des Finances. What gave Vaux-le-Vicomte its special character was its interior decoration, which was conceived as a whole by Charles Le Brun (1619–90) and executed by his team of fine craftsmen. It was a totally French achievement, created and carried out entirely by Frenchmen. Vaux was a resounding success, one that we can still admire today. It was too much so even for the owner. The king loved it, but became very jealous. He could not allow a courtier to surpass his splendor. So, in 1661, Fouquet was arrested and charged with embezzlement. *Quelle surprise!*

Shortly after, Le Brun and his team were engaged in the royal service. Le Brun's first major work of interior decoration for the king was the Galerie d'Apollon at the Château du Louvre. His greatest achievement, however, is the interior design and decoration of the famed Château de Versailles. Le Brun is responsible for creating and firmly setting up the grandeur and magnificence, which became associated with the Sun King. He established the French style, creating the ultimate model, which was so admired from then on that it became the standard for aristocratic interior decoration. Soon, all of Europe followed suit.

Why did this create such a stir? Why would so many want to copy this style? First, it was much more than just a style. It was a way of life—a luxurious, coordinated, and structured way of life that happened to be beautiful to look at and was comfortable to live in (for the time). Good interior design has to reflect and enhance a way of life, and indeed Le Brun's approach did so. Good decoration is integrated throughout the home, with its

architecture and gardens, which are not just a mere theatrical backdrop. It reflects an intellectual, refined society, populated with sophisticated and fashionable people.

There is more. Otherwise, all that luxury would have been stifling and boring—and God forbid, the worst sin in that ultrasophisticated society was to be a bore. Wit is an essential ingredient. It is the secret that makes the whole thing come alive and sing: the masses of feathers on top of the bed in the bedchamber, the Sun King's red heels, the masterfully carved and gilded dog's chairs, the extravagantly shaped topiaries in the otherwise orderly gardens, the omnipresent orange trees growing in greenhouses (at a time when there was no central heating, this was no small feat), the total fantasy of the Chambre des Amours in the Pavillon de Porcelaine, the myriad embroidered cushions for the barges on the canals at Versailles, and the red *roulette* for the king to allow him to be wheeled in the garden, alongside his courtiers. The list could go on and on.

Style resides in the extra detail and the quirkiness that slightly pushes the envelope, showing that you are in the know and that you are slightly detached. It is, I suppose, the ultimate snob appeal, the ultimate insider joke. However, in order to pull it off, you have to be supremely confident in your own taste. Therefore, you have to be knowledgeable. It is where the famous mix of high and low that the French are known for comes from. This is the essence of French style.

Speaking about high and low, it is often forgotten that in addition to the grand public rooms of Versailles, which are imposing and stately as they should be, there were many private rooms in which the king and members of the royal family could relax. For example, just below the Grand Appartement was a luxury flat known as the Appartement des Bains, which comprised a sumptuous bathroom (a great novelty for the time) and a suite of rooms where Louis XIV and his favorite (of the moment), Madame de Montespan, spent many happy hours in private.

On all levels, Versailles marked a turning point in the evolution of design. It not only set the stage for royal performances for centuries to come, but it also established a certain standard of living, behaving, and entertaining. From then on, to have beautiful dwellings enhanced with fine comfortable furniture upholstered *en suite*, rare collections, and gardens to match, became the signs of a cultivated man or woman, *une personne de qualité*.

The standard of living trickled down to all levels of society and was adopted by each according to his or her means. A plan for luxurious living in palaces was established. Classical symmetry was the main motto. Therefore, an important house from the 1670s onward was entered via a hall, which was no longer used for dining (as in the Middle Ages), leading to a grand staircase where architects began to display much creativity, up through a *salon*, a withdrawing room, an antechamber (the room before the bedroom) to the bedchamber (fancy bedroom, rarely used for sleeping) with its great display bed and small,

A painting by Jean Baptiste Charpentier showing the Duc de Penthièvre (1725–93) and his daughter, the future Duchesse d'Orléans, on a bench in a garden at Versailles. Photo: RMN.

necessary private rooms beyond—closets, *garde-robes*, and dressing rooms. Of course, architects were busy creating variations on the theme during the following centuries. I possess some first-hand knowledge of this, having lived for quite a few years in a place called Château de Plassac, which was built around 1780 and has a very similar floor plan. What is remarkable is that the succession of rooms opening into one another makes for a very gracious living, and that the scale of each room is extremely comfortable and in sync with human scale despite the overall large size of the building (which is certainly not the case with many of the "McMansions" of today). The architect was

ABOVE: Aerial view of the Château de Plassac designed by Victor Louis, the architect of the city of Bordeaux and the Palais Royal in Paris.

OPPOSITE: Design for a ceiling of the Théâtre Français, Paris, by Aimé Chenavard. The Metropolitan Museum of Art, The Elisha Whittelsey Fund, 1958.

Victor Louis (1731–1800), who is famous for erecting the Grand Théâtre in Bordeaux, after over two hundred years still the most magnificent theater in France. Another one of his masterpieces is the Palais Royal in Paris, which dates from the same period.

A similar master plan repeated itself in many French castles as well as those abroad. Each room in this sequence was more elegant than the next. Anyone going through the doors would find the decor increasingly beautiful, culminating in the ultimate splendor of the bedchamber or bedroom. This arrangement was done for maximum effect, where rooms opened *en enfilade* (meaning that rooms were arranged in a line so the connecting French doors followed one another and you could look right down the whole row). This kind of perspective was one of the most magnificent effects. For most of the eighteenth and even into the nineteenth century, it became the most common arrangement. The doorway was placed close to the window so that the main part of the room lay on one side as one proceeded along the line. Usually the fireplace was set in the middle of the wall facing someone entering the *enfilade*.

Once the ground plan was worked out, the architect concentrated his attention on the inside of the building's interior. The proportion of each room was treated as a separate spatial unit, and the doors, windows, fireplace, and moldings were carefully spaced in harmonious arrangement. A room's proportions were, and still are, a vital element. Ceiling height usually varied between 14 to 18 feet, depending whether the room was to be used for ceremonial purposes or not. Grand ceilings sometimes had gilded elements—crowns, coronets, and ribbons binding festoons and wreaths. Painted decoration and *trompe l'oeil* imitations of plasterwork ceilings, inspired by Le Brun, were other ways to accentuate the effect—the formality, importance, or coziness, depending on its function. Great care was also given to the walls, which were finished with carved wood paneling, medallions, and over-door and over-mantel panels, which were sometimes enhanced with gilding, or simply with multiple paint accents as well as crown moldings and chair rails.

The all-important fireplace (do not forget that it was the only source of heat at the time) was given preferential treatment. It was always heavily decorated and carved. Architects spent a great deal of time and effort creating designs for chimneypieces. A book by Jean Barbet, *Livre d'Architecture*, first published in 1632 and dedicated to Cardinal Richelieu, attempted to show *ce qu'il y a de beau dans Paris*. It illustrated many variations of chimney designs that were circulated throughout European courts. These designs were widely copied, and Barbet's tome was so popular that it was reprinted in 1642. He was not the only designer by any means—Jean Le Pautre (1618–82), a French Baroque designer and one of the creators of the Louis XIV style, shared his master Le Brun's taste for sober magnificence, and his almost two thousand known engraved designs provide unique guidance. In 1665, he published several sets of drawings reflecting the new tendency toward a lower and smaller fireplace opening (resulting in a less drafty room) and a generally less massive fireplace. A breakthrough in lighting the chimneypiece was introduced around 1684 in the new Chambre du Roi at Versailles by means of a mirror glass above the mantel. From then on, mirrors above mantels became the latest French taste.

Of course, floors are the base of the architectural and design effect. Fine floor *parquet à la française* (laid in squares) became the favorite material for the main rooms. Noteworthy are the careful instructions given for the laying of the intricate marquetry floor in the Petite Galerie at Versailles in 1685. More than a dozen different kinds of woods were to be laid over a complete new sub-floor of ancient oak boards and no singeing or dyeing was to be used.

An extra level of sophistication needed to be added to most floors at Versailles. This is told by eyewitness Nicodemus Tessin (1654–1728) who traveled from Sweden to France to observe all the beauties and novelties of Versailles. As the Architecte Royal for the Swedish kings Charles XI and then Charles XII, he was responsible for the French beautification of Sweden. Tessin was a great admirer of Louis XIV, and of the way he used the decorative arts to reinforce his power. Tessin reported that in 1693 at Versailles all rooms but one had parquet laid *en lozenges* (diagonally). He then duly copied this flooring for the Royal Château in Stockholm. From then on (even to this day), this type of marquetry floor is called in the trade *parquet de Versailles.*

Due to a certain practicality, suitability, and elegance, marble or limestone became the obligatory materials of choice for entrances, hallways, and stairs. So, even the floor's treatment became codified. Once the architectural shell was erected, the interior had to be furnished.

As I have already mentioned, Le Brun, a painter by training, was the creative genius behind the decorating schemes first at Vaux-le-Vicomte and then at the French royal palaces, among which Versailles stands out as the crowning glory. Already at Vaux he had provided sketches for individual pieces of furniture—an unusual practice at the time—which the various craftsmen would make. When, in 1663, he was appointed the first director of the Manufacture des Gobelins (that incredible group of workshops, staffed by the most talented craftsmen of the day), he continued this practice. He not only painted cartoons for *tapisseries* (tapestries), but also provided designs for them, and supervised the work of the goldsmiths, *ébénistes,* cabinetmakers, carvers, gilders, and bronze workers. This led to the notion that architects would design the furniture that was in keeping with the architecture. In other words, it all had to be part of a whole. Such architects as the father and son Jean and Daniel Marot, for example, published design books depicting what was called "architectural furniture," which included state beds, chairs, benches, candlesticks and candle stands, side tables, and consoles. Such designs became an essential tool in spreading French taste abroad. New pieces of furniture continued to be created. Records show that the first *commodes* (chests of drawers) with four drawers, were delivered to Versailles in May 1692. Like the *armoire* (wardrobe), which also appeared on the scene in the 1690s, the *commode* fulfilled the need for a more comfortable life, one in which fashion and its many accessories play a part.

The *armoire* and the *commode* both seem to have been the brainchild of yet another talented protégé of Louis XIV and of Le Brun—André-Charles Boulle (1642–1732). The first great French *ébéniste* and the most celebrated of the king's furniture-makers, he created the technique that became known as Boulle marquetry. It is done by gluing together sheets of brass and tortoiseshell, which are then cut according to a design. Either brass or tortoiseshell are used as a background and then reversed. Pairs of *armoires* or *commodes* can then be decorated; one with a brass ground with tortoiseshell on top and the other with the reverse. To obtain an even richer effect, the brass was often engraved. In addition, the parts of the pieces that were not decorated with Boulle marquetry were usually veneered with ebony. The effect was dazzling. Boulle worked continuously for the royal palaces, especially at Versailles where his design for the Dauphin's *grand cabinet* (c. 1681–83, now destroyed) was considered a masterpiece. Boulle's furniture, in addition to his exceptional marquetry, is distinguished by the monumentality of its architectural forms and by the outstanding quality of its gilt bronze mounts.

Gilding and gilt become synonymous with classic French taste. Louis XIV and his royal cabinetmakers invented the quintessential look—sparkling objects and furniture that could hold their own when surrounded by the wattage of a thousand candles and the acreage of mirrors that brightened dinners at Versailles. Boulle became acclaimed throughout Europe and was widely copied—this being the best form of flattery, as we know. Later in the eighteenth century, he published a series of engraved designs, *Nouveaux Desseins de Meubles et Ouvrages de Bronze et de Menuiserie, inventés et gravés par A-C Boulle, Paris.* Enthralled by the quality and magnificence of Boulle's furniture, Philippe V of Spain and the Electors of Bavaria and Cologne ordered many pieces. Civilized living was very much on the agenda for furniture as well, and the French who were supreme masters in the creation of comfortable pieces, invented small tables for taking meals in bed. Inventories tell us that there were six tables *pour servir à manger sur le lit* at the Château de Marly, a royal residence where informality and relaxation was *de rigueur.*

The numerous printed drawings and designs became valuable and easily accessible sources of inspiration and reference for foreign craftsmen to turn to. Another way French taste expanded outside its borders was through the lavish gifts from the Sun King himself to various foreign ambassadors, such as the state bed and matching suite of chairs and stools that he gave the Swedish count Nils Bielke. These pieces were intended to display French splendor. It was marketing at its best and it worked!

To finish a room and make it as comfortable as possible, carpets, fabric, and upholstery were needed. Initially the French in their continuous search for luxury were fascinated with weavings from the Orient. But in order to counterbalance such imports, the Savonnerie, which would become the most important European factory of knotted pile carpets, was created after many false starts. Founded by Louis XIII in 1627, its name comes from the fact that the factory was housed in an old soap works—hence the name on the Quai de Chaillot, in Paris.

The Savonnerie's most impressive period was during the beginning of Louis XIV's reign when a magnificent series of carpets was commissioned for the Galerie d'Apollon at Versailles. These carpets probably the finest ever made in Europe, have a fine, close, woolen pile tied with special knots. They were woven on upright looms similar to those used for tapestries. The factory would go on to produce many fine carpets in the Empire style, well into the nineteenth century and the Second Empire. The other interesting point is it continued to make wall hangings (which is how wall decoration started in the first place) and in the early twentieth century panels were produced after paintings by Monet, Manet, and van Gogh.

Since the Middle Ages, fabrics such as *tapisseries* and wall hangings were a good way to warm a room. However, because they were moved from place to place along with the few pieces of furniture needed, nothing matched in any way, shape, or form. Once again, we have to wait until the

André-Charles Boulle (1642–1732) was the first great French *ébéniste*. Boulle's work perfectly embodied his period's taste for grand style. His name is associated with a type of ornate tortoiseshell and brass marquetry, as seen on these chairs.

Projet d'un Tapis pour le Sallon pour être éxéca

LEFT AND ABOVE: Jean-François Bélanger (1744–1818) is the designer of these carpet studies. The carpet at left was to be executed in England. The example above was intended for a large *galerie* in the Hôtel Mazarin and was to be made by the Manufacture de la Savonnerie. The Metropolitan Museum of Art, Harris Brisbane Dick Fund, 1932.

time of Louis XIV to see furniture upholstered *en suite*, enhanced by the color of the walls and curtains—the beginning of a unified decorative scheme.

The first to create a unified decorative scheme was Madame de Rambouillet (1588–1665). In 1619, she famously amazed the sophisticated world when she set about redecorating her father's Parisian *hôtel particulier* (a free-standing private house) in a design that involved not only painting all the walls shades of blue but also having all the furnishings, including wall hangings, bed hangings, window curtains, and carpets, woven in variations of blue and gold to match! It was a novel idea. The changes that this highly intelligent woman, who ran a famous literary salon, made in her house came to occupy an important place in the history of interior decoration. Madame de Rambouillet and her circle showed the way to ease, comfort, and civilized living in the first quarter of the seventeenth century.

The last quarter of that century saw her ideas carried to perfection within the orbit of the Sun King at Versailles, where the walls and doors were hung with matching fabrics. Chairs were also matching and the same fabric was hung on the bed. For the first time walls were covered with fixed hangings, such as the delicately executed one for the Grande Galerie at Versailles, which was described as *une tenture de tapisserie peinte sur un fond de toile d'argent trait, representant partie de l'histoire du Roy, dessin de Mr. Le Brun.*

Walls were covered not only with *tapisseries* but also with woven damask, silk, brocade, and brocatelle. Early on, Louis XIV had established the silk industry in Lyons, whose looms produced smooth silk, taffetas, *moirés*, satins, and fringes of all sorts. By 1730, the first naturalistic patterns were introduced, and major improvements in the technique of preparing and weaving silk was accomplished. All of this would be a great help to the upholsterer. The appearance of a late seventeenth- or eighteenth-century room depended also on the contribution made by upholsterers who provided all the hangings—for beds, windows, and walls—as well as the covering for chairs. Sofas and chairs were often done in Savonnerie *en suite* with carpet or precious silk in coordinated color schemes. The upholsterer also knew where to find trimmings of all kinds to finish the effect, very much as today, when you think of it. Trimming was very important and served a dual purpose, at the time as it still does. It was used to finish off edges of upholstery work and to hide the seams as well as to add a superb embellishment. Trim was everywhere, even on the cushions of boats sailing down the canals at Versailles. According to the royal inventory, all were equipped with luxurious cushions in colors matching those of the boat: in the *felouque Napolitaine violette*, for example, there were *cinq carreaux de damas garnis chacun de gallon et de quatre glands d'argent, avec housse de serge violette*. What an utter luxury!

Failings were well hidden by lavish trimmings, or *passementeries*. The variety of trimmings was very diverse. They encompassed a large spectrum of fringes of all lengths, rosettes, tassels, braid, galloons, cords, ribbon, and lace, each of them bearing their own name. Trimming was an art indeed and the special job of the *passementier* who worked hand in hand with the upholsterer. It is not surprising that some late seventeenth-

century upholsterers became rich and famous. Simon de Lobel, the principal *tapissier* to Louis XIV, was a household name in France around 1680, and Capin, the royal *tapissier* for Louis XVI, made a small fortune.

Drawing of the stern of *La Réal* (detail), a boat (*grande gondole*) on the canal at Versailles. The Metropolitan Museum of Art, Rogers Fund, 1965.

Suitability and comfort was then and continued to be the hallmark of French style, as Edith Wharton so rightly proclaimed, in *French Ways and Their Meaning*, 1919, saying: *The essence of taste is suitability.* Throughout the nineteenth century and during the twentieth, architecture, design, and interior decoration—based on the classical principles and the philosophy established at the end of the seventeenth century—changed, following society and its evolving way of life. Even during the tumultuous Art Nouveau and Art Deco periods, the same principles of comfort and suitability were still *de rigueur*.

We have to wait until Le Corbusier (born Charles-Edouard Jeanneret; 1887–1965) arrives on the scene to see architecture and interior design take a radically different turn for a brief moment. He viewed architecture as a support for a way of life that appealed to him. With such a philosophy he did not differ from his classical ancestors; however, his vision of life was very stark, to say the least. What can you expect—the man came from Switzerland! Yes, he was not exactly French. It might be his excuse for his puritan view of life, which was distinctly not Gallic!

For Le Corbusier, the function of a house was in his own words to provide: *1. A shelter against heat, cold, rain, thieves, and the inquisitive. 2. A receptacle for light and sun. 3. A certain number of cells appropriated to cooking,*

work, and personal life. For him, a house was *une machine à habiter* (a machine to live in). We are miles away from a cozy, comforting place and yet his desire was to create a beautiful, safe, spiritual haven that was for him the essence of modernity. Intellectually you could make a case for it. However, human beings are not robots who can be parked in a sterile cell. Technically it was a disaster. Flat roofs are a recipe for failure in rainy or snowy countries. The Villa Savoye, built in 1929 outside Paris, in Poissy, had leaky roofs. In the words of its owners: *It's raining in the hall, it's raining on the ramp, and the wall of the garage is absolutely soaked. What's more, it's still raining in my bathroom, which floods in bad weather, as the water comes in through the skylight.* In a nutshell, the house was totally uninhabitable! World War II saved Le Corbusier from a costly lawsuit by the enraged owners.

The concept of the house was a large step toward the future and the essence of modernity, maybe too large of a step at the time and certainly quite the opposite concept of the luxury embraced during the previous centuries, and yet only rich collectors could afford the stark simplicity of Le Corbusier, despite his claim. However, it was creative—constant creativity is also one of the hallmarks of French style. Suitability— where is it when you need it? It was one important element, which was lacking in Le Corbusier's plan despite his genius. Luckily, it soon returned with the architects and designers of the 1940s. French style was back again on its comfortable, refined track.

Among the many prolific and talented creators of that period are Jacques Adnet, Jean Royère, Jules Leleu, and André Arbus, to name a few. Arbus (1903–69), the son of a cabinetmaker, had the passion of a visionary and the instinctual understanding of the symbiotic relationship between art, architecture, and furniture design, continuing the long tradition of French style at its best. He clearly strove to be innovative without breaking with tradition because he believed that, the artistic works of the past, beyond their perfection, bear witness to man's effort toward truth. Arbus also felt that home design and furniture is successful only when it has been conceived on a human scale—that a chair, for example, must be designed to contain the human body and that home decor must embody the comfort and harmony indicative of the human spirit.

In describing a child's room designed by André Arbus, Waldemar Georges writes in 1937 in *L'Art Vivant*: *An impression of clarity, honesty, moral distinction and gentleness of living emanates from this ensemble. In conceiving and creating* La Maison d'une famille Française, *which is neither a counter-shock nor a counter-revolution in the domain of the decorative arts but represents a tangible witness of the eternal youth of French art, Arbus finally ends with the struggle between beauty and utility, art and the people.* Arbus became well known for his versatility, which was amply illustrated by his double participation at L'Exposition Internationale des Arts et Techniques dans la Vie Moderne in Paris, held in 1937. On one side he shows *La Maison d'une famille Française* for a middle income family and on the other side he presents *Une demeure en Ile-de-France*, in which he gives *libre cours* to his imagination, a sense of luxury, and even adds a touch of surrealism. During World War II, back in his hometown of Toulouse, he created the decor of Marcelle Alix's fashion house, using for his inspiration the pleats *à l'antique* of her dresses for curtains and trim. After the war, the French President Vincent Auriol commissioned Arbus to create decors for the Château de Rambouillet and the Elysée Palace. In so doing Auriol followed the *dirigisme* in art of the *Ancient Régime*.

The same thing happened to Philippe Starck in 1982, when his career began in earnest and he was asked to design the private interiors for French president François Mitterrand. Philippe Patrick Starck (born in

1949) has created large, spectacular interiors as well as mass-produced consumer goods as mundane as toothbrushes or as ubiquitous as chairs, always bringing a sense of humor and carrying through historical references in a tongue-in-cheek manner. The Louis Ghost armchair is a perfect example. If Louis XV was alive, he would want a chair like that made of molded transparent plastic.

A sense of humor and suitability—in the words of Edith Wharton, *comfort, quality, a certain sense of historical tradition*—allied with endless creativity, strong individuality, and a dash of quirkiness, make the recipe for the special *je ne sais quoi* that characterizes French design. It is alive, well, and kicking. Just read on. It is easier than it seems. *Bonne chance, amusez-vous bien.* First, you have to realize that creating your home is *un plaisir.* Make the process fun and you will feel rewarded and fulfilled. Remember Voltaire's description of the *Temple du Gout:*

> *Noble et tranquille, son architecture s'elève;*
> *Chaque ornement dans la bonne position,*
> *Comme si la nécessité l'avait placé là:*
> *L'art trompe en volant l'air de la nature,*
> *L'oeil avec plaisir saisie toute sa structure,*
> *Jamais surpris, et toujours content.*
> (Noble and plain its architecture rose;
> Each ornament in due position shows,
> As if necessity had set it there:
> There art deceives by stealing nature's air,
> The eye with pleasure all its structure seized,
> Never astonished, and yet always pleased.)

OPPOSITE: Detail of the blue salon, with a card table set up, designed by Madeleine Castaing (1894–1992) for her Parisian apartment on rue Jacob. She believed in having rooms ready at all times for different activities. Photo: Antoine Bootz.

ABOVE: The legendary decorator Madeleine Castaing was a great inspiration to me. Written in lipstick on the mirror is the playful greeting from writer François-Marie Banier, *Where are you going, Beautiful?* Photo: Antoine Bootz.

A French-American Stylish Affair

Mr. Franklin has been so long in France that he is more of a Frenchman than an American.
I doubt whether he will enjoy himself perfectly if he returns to America.
—John Quincy Adams (1767–1848), quoted in 1785

JACQUELINE KENNEDY, our most charismatic and glamorous First Lady, embraced French culture. She set out to make the White House under her guidance an "American Versailles." Jackie spoke the language (her grandparents were French) and served French food, wine, and Champagne for elegant state dinners. Under her tutelage, the White House got a complete makeover. Coordinating the effort to restore America's most treasured home was a Frenchman, Stephan Boudin, the president of the Paris decorating firm Jansen. The most fashionable French decorators of the mid-twentieth century, Boudin numbered among his clients the Duke and Duchess of Windsor.

Jackie's taste and style, unlike any other First Lady's, took on an almost mythic dimension and holds its fascination to this day. With her love of French culture, she was not unlike our founding fathers. In America the attraction to France is hardly new. The historical links are deep despite the sometimes love-hate relationship between the two countries.

The inspiration for lofty, sophisticated, and cool surroundings seems to have originated in France. Style, as we know it, began in France too. So did decoration on a grand, coordinated scale. France, under the Sun King, Louis XIV, became a beacon for entertainment, food, fashion, design, and architecture in the seventeenth century. Louis XIV set out to elevate his court to the highest level of sophistication in order to limit the demand for imports of luxury goods from abroad, to tie the rebellious aristocracy to his golden chariot, and outshine every other power in the Western world.

Louis XIV's capable minister, Colbert, contributed to the effort by creating the Gobelins (also known as the Manufacture

Louis XIV, who carefully cultivated his image as the Sun King, fittingly dances the role of Apollo, god of the sun, for the ballet *La Nuit,* 1653, at age fourteen. Bibliothèque Nationale de France.

Royale de la Couronne). Its foundation coincided with strict rules for running the Garde-Meuble. The talented craftsmen who were skilled enough to win a place were given, in addition to large salaries, such privileges as free education for their children. The list of furniture, clocks, and objects made during that period is mind-boggling: sets of silver and gold chairs and consoles, for example, which subsequently were melted down in 1689 in order to pay for the War of the League of Augsburg of 1688 to 1697 and the War of the Spanish Succession of 1702 to 1713. It is interesting to note that the king personally ordered much of the work. He was shown wax figures for approval. The Gobelins was swiftly followed by the creation of carpet and tapestry factories at Aubusson and Beauvais, production of silk at Lyons, lace and embroideries at Alençon, Chantilly, and Le Havre, and glass at the royal factory in Saint Gobain.

The decorating of the Galerie des Glaces at Versailles, beginning in 1679, is enough evidence of the king's success. From then on, French style was "it." A refined *art de vivre* had been created. Decor functioned as a necessary backdrop to a high quality of life. At the time, French artists made engravings of exquisite settings for witty encounters among sophisticated beings and lovely backdrops for celebrated beauties that were assembled in books on interior decoration. This way of living was exported throughout Europe and the Americas.

To this day, France continues to be a leader in high design style and entertainment. The finest silks were woven, cotton and linen were printed, and toile de Jouy was invented. Fine upholstery techniques were practiced. Delicate Sèvres porcelain and silver were used for dinner; both served as a fitting display for exotic culinary delights. Exquisite Aubusson carpets muffled the noise and kept out the cold. The luxury-goods market created by the French was here to stay.

The ties between America and France ran deep from the start. Thomas Jefferson and Benjamin Franklin, two giants of American history who returned from visits to France shortly before the start of the French Revolution, brought back crates of objects, furniture, and books, in addition to many ideas for the newly conceived America. Both were infatuated with everything French.

Jefferson's five-year stay in Paris made him a complete Francophile, despite the fact that he did not quite master the language. When he returned from France, his furnishings and household goods filled eighty-six packing crates. Their contents revealed that during his stay in the French capital he had engaged in an epic shopping binge that included the purchase of fifty-seven chairs, two sofas, six large mirrors, wallpaper, silver, china, linen, clocks, and scientific equipment. Kitchen equipment, including several French stoves, French art, books, and wines were also among his purchases. When Jefferson returned to America, he was acknowledged to be such a wine

The dining room at Monticello, Thomas Jefferson's (1743–1826) house in Virginia. The decoration of this room shows Jefferson's taste for French Neoclassical in his choice of urns and classical figures on the mantel and mirror as well as the French Louis XVI-style armchairs in front of the fireplace. Monticello/Thomas Jefferson Foundation Inc.

expert that he served as a wine adviser to three presidents—Washington, Madison, and Monroe. During his own presidency, he purchased and served French wines on an extravagant scale. He even helped make Champagne fashionable in Washington by serving it at most of his state dinners.

I cannot live without books, Jefferson once famously wrote. *Old French books out of which he fishes everything,* bitterly complained his architect, Benjamin Henry Latrobe, when Thomas Jefferson rejected his initial designs for the president's house in Washington, D.C. It was obviously lacking the requisite French touch.

Benjamin Franklin, during the eight and a half years he lived outside Paris, enjoyed a very social and active life. He entertained a great deal and despite his age charmed his neighbors. He became smitten by Anne Catherine de Liginville, Madame Helvetius. In 1779, at the ripe age of seventy, he asked the aristocratic lady to marry him. Similarly, France fell in love with Franklin. He was hailed as a hero; admiring crowds would gather outside his residence, passersby in the street cheered the "good doctor." Fashionable Parisian women even took to wearing a variation of his familiar bearskin hat. A mutual admiration society had begun.

Upon his arrival to France, John Adams noted in his diary how much it surprised him to find France so appealing. Adams unexpectedly found that he too loved the French and their approach to life—despite

Monticello is the work of a lifetime. The parlor and living room (*salon*) reflect a strong French Neoclassical influence, including a harpsichord, which Jefferson brought back from Paris. The French seating further contribute to the sophisticated elegance. Dai Hirota / Impact Photographics.

Adjacent to his bedroom suite, Jefferson had an indoor-outdoor space that functioned as a greenhouse. Monticello/Thomas Jefferson Foundation Inc.

the fact that their lifestyle ran counter to his Puritan upbringing. *If human nature could be made happy by anything that can please the eye, the ear, the taste or any other sense, or passion or fancy, this country would be the region for happiness,* wrote Adams. *The delights of France are innumerable. The politeness, the elegance, the softness, the delicacy is extreme.*

Even General George Washington succumbed to the French influence. On April 30, 1789, Washington took the oath of office as the first American president. Tradition states that he stood outside on the balcony of Federal Hall (a French-inspired Neoclassical building) at the intersection of Wall and Broad Streets in New York. The architect Pierre Charles L'Enfant renovated City Hall and renamed it Federal Hall for the occasion. A native of France, he had trained at the Ecole des Beaux Arts. Later L'Enfant served as an engineer under Washington during the American Revolution, and eventually designed the Baroque master plan for Washington, D.C. Today, a few pieces of the earliest documented American furniture in the Neoclassical style, with details borrowed directly from the Louis XVI style, still remain in this building that housed the First Congress. These armchairs, side chairs, desks, and two sofas were intended to symbolize the emergence of a new nation. In fact, the French design characteristics of early Federal furniture are reflections of the cultural aspirations of the first American leaders. So, *quid pro quo*.

It was not uncommon at the time to consider the French desire for democratic liberty a natural outgrowth of the French experience in the American Revolution. Maybe it was also a way for our forerunners to justify the extent of their French infatuation. Culture and style is a French staple, and countless artists, writers, and politicians throughout centuries have felt that way. For Hemingway, *Paris is a movable feast*. For Gertrude Stein, *America is my country, Paris is my hometown*. And for Oscar Wilde, *When good Americans die they go to Paris, and when bad Americans die, where do they go to? Oh, they go to America*.

Which brings up an important point. The French way of doing things does not necessarily mean that you need to be a Rockefeller to afford it. Anyone can decorate his or her home with the right direction. You do express yourself in your home whether you intend to or not. Elsie de Wolfe (1865–1950), a *grande dame* of American interior design, deeply believed in this philosophy and the art of homemaking. She took great inspiration from French design. Living part of the year in Versailles, at the Villa Trianon, a stone's throw away from the Sun King's great palace, she spent the rest of the year in New York at the Irving House, an American version of a European salon. Here, de Wolf held soirées that attracted a wide range of international visitors such as Sarah Bernhardt, Oscar Wilde, and J. P. Morgan. Her interiors contributed partially to her social success; they were mostly furnished with pieces brought back from France, many in the Louis XVI style that were painted white. She cited that her design inspirations came largely from French style in her widely successful book *The House in Good Taste*. Through her commercial work, including New York's Colony Club, de Wolf created a faithful following of aficionados. Edith Wharton (1861–1937), another major Francophile, lived in France, bought French furniture, and peppered *The Decoration of Houses* with French historical references. Both books are iconic. Full of wit and humor, they treat interior decoration as a necessity for a beautiful life— a helpful background for success—while amply crediting decorative history, mainly French. In such genteel, pulled-together, surroundings the *douceur de vivre* of the French-American way of life comes through. It is a very important point. The key word here is *vivre*—it means "living." For both de Wolfe and Wharton, decoration is all about a better, sweeter life where the decor is the springboard, a backdrop for *une certaine qualité de vie*.

We are not talking here about picture-perfect houses, which only look good in glossy magazines, but vibrant, comfortable spaces that will enhance your everyday life. This sums up my philosophy: Beautiful surroundings need to be appropriate to the place and role they are supposed to serve. Historical knowledge, common sense, and a healthy dose of wit and humor need to be added to the mix. *Voilà*.

This book sets out to show how by following in the footsteps of Elsie de Wolfe and Edith Wharton you can create elegant but comfortable surroundings that will enhance your life and the lives of your friends and family *à la française*. Moreover, you can have fun doing it!

OPPOSITE: The library at the Mount, Edith Wharton's house, showing her extensive collection of books. Photo: David Dashiell/The Mount.

ABOVE: The Mount in the Massachusetts Berkshires, viewed from the garden. Photo: David Dashiell/The Mount.

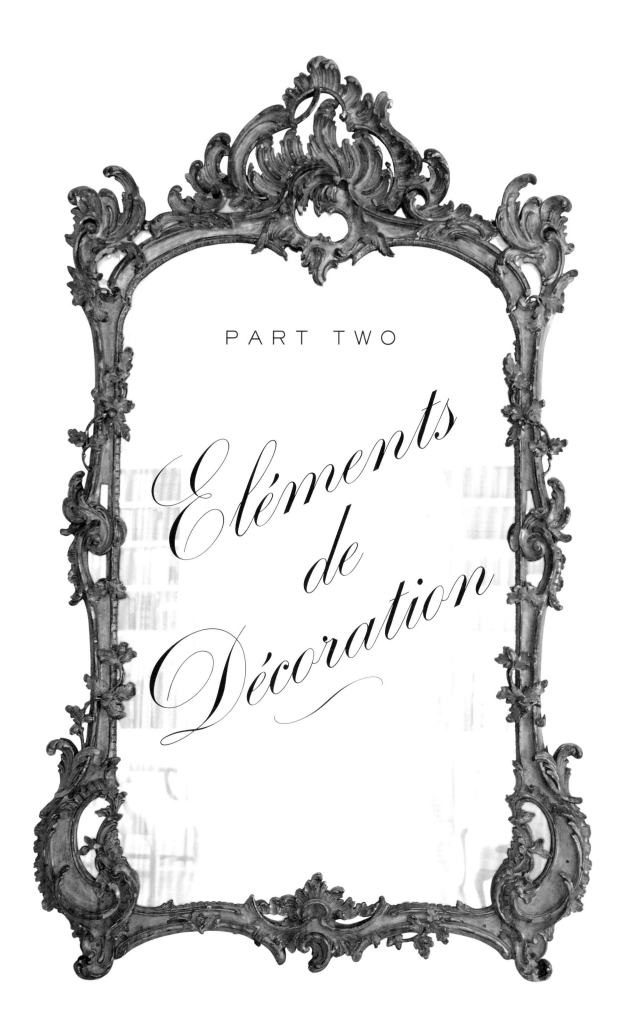

PART TWO

Eléments de Décoration

Floor Plan,
Ceilings & Floors

La symétrie, base de la composition architecturale, consiste en l'accord de mesure entre les différents éléments de l'oeuvre, comme entre les éléments séparés et l'ensemble—comme dans le corps humain.

(Symmetry is the basis of architectural compositions. It consists of an agreement between the measurements of all the different elements—like in the human body.)

—Vitruvius (first century A.D.)

FLOOR PLAN

Important French buildings, from the Château du Louvre to Chambord, were designed by architects for whom the ancient principles of symmetry were very important. Early building designs consisted of a ground plan (*le plan*) and elevations based on such simple geometric shapes as a square. As early as the sixteenth century the French published engraved plans in books on architecture. Philibert de l'Orme produced a nearly complete volume, *Le Premier Tome d'Architecture*, in 1567.

The most famous opus was Jacques Androuet du Cerceau's *Les plus excellents bâstiments de France*, published in two volumes, c. 1576 and 1579. The interest in this subject was so great that papers and books were produced in Paris in ever-growing quantities. They included not only floor plans but also furniture, fireplaces, and other components of interiors.

A plethora of French books on architecture became widely known in the seventeenth century. Most of these publications focused on architecture and covered such basic elements as the classical

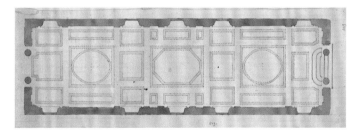

PAGE 46: Niches, door frames, cornices, and moldings are helpful finishing touches. Their architectural quality becomes even more visible when painted a different color than the walls.

OPPOSITE: François Joseph Bélanger, Study for the dining room ceiling of the Pavillon de Bagatelle (detail). The Metropolitan Museum of Art, Harris Brisbane Dick Fund, 1932.

ABOVE: This drawing is of an elongated room, possibly a chapel but more likely a gallery. It is inscribed in French: *Projet de Chaire de Versailles*. National Museum, Stockholm.

orders, facades, doors, pediments, and ground plans. They were an endless resource for designing doors, windows, and practical arrangements for rooms, and even included instructions on how to build an icehouse. The most popular titles included Pierre Le Muet's *Manière de bien bâtir pour touttes sortes de personnes*, 1623, Roland Fréart's *Parallèle de l'architecture antique et de la moderne*, 1650, and Jean Marot's *L'Architecture François ou recueil des plans bâtis dans Paris et ses environs*, c. 1670.

What is so striking about seventeenth- and eighteenth-century plans is that they are so orderly and balanced, as well as being beautiful. Proportion was considered a key element of successful design. Indeed, many of these early renderings were so popular that they were distributed in London and Amsterdam. These designed rooms had struck the right balance.

Chic Advice

My mantra is to try to simplify things. The best way to do this is to find the tools that will make a task easier. A floor plan is an excellent tool. It will help you visualize the configuration of your house. You will notice proportional imperfections such as walls that are narrower than others or a fireplace that is slightly off center. Practically speaking, it is nearly impossible to carry out a successful interior design project without a floor plan. (Besides, it is certainly much easier on your back to move furniture on paper!) The floor plan will act as the ultimate organizer.

◆ Begin by sketching a floor plan, noting the dimensions of the walls. If one wall is longer than the other, make it longer on your paper. If you do not own a scale ruler and want to create an accurate plan, an ordinary ruler is a fine substitute. Use this simple rule of thumb for scaling measurements: one quarter inch equals one foot. My advice is to keep the following in mind. Try to determine the traffic pattern of the room that you are working on. Decide if there are any doors that you want to block off, as well as in what direction you want traffic to flow. Rooms should not become obstacle courses. Any doors that you intend to use should have a clear passage. You will also need to determine the activity zone and where the major seating area will be placed.

◆ Always start by deciding where to place the big pieces of furniture: the bed in the bedroom, the sofas in the sitting room, the dining table in the dining room. This will make it easier to determine the positioning of the rest of the furniture.

◆ The way light falls naturally in a space often dictates how and where the furniture should be placed. Remember, too, that it is more pleasant to be seated in a room when you are in a sunny spot or can see the view.

◆ One of the major reasons room designs can turn out to be failures is a lack of a focal point. Plan a room with a focal point in mind; it will anchor your space and give it direction. A fireplace or a great view make excellent focal points. Be sure that the living room sofa faces a focal point and that the bed is the focus in the bedroom.

◆ Never underestimate the importance of proper lighting. When the final furniture arrangements are made, you will need to determine where to place the lights. That's why it is important to indicate the location of outlets on your floor plan.

◆ After following these guidelines, you will need to make some adjustments to your design scheme. The floor plan will save you considerable time and effort (as well as strain on your back).

CEILINGS

One of the most noticeable features of a room in seventeenth-century France was the ceiling (*plafond*), and architects gave much thought to creating striking ceilings. Let us just say that here too the French published many designs to assist architects. Elaborate plasterwork ceilings were the norm in most palaces and were often enhanced by beautiful painted decorations. Grander ceilings had gilded elements (*rehaussé d'or sur fond blanc*), crowns and coronets, ribbons, festoons, and wreaths, such as those designed by Jean Bérain (1637–1711) for the Hôtel de Mailly. Bérain was yet another proponent of the Louis XIV style. Beginning in 1670 he was employed by the Crown as an engraver, and in 1674 became *Dessinateur de la Chambre et du Cabinet du Roi*. When Charles Le Brun's (1619–90) star waned at court, Bérain's rose, and on Le Brun's death he became chief designer. His designs for furniture, ceilings, *boiseries* (woodwork), and *cheminées* (fireplaces) were published as engravings. Many of his creations are light, elegant, and whimsical; these decorations hover on the brink of the fanciful Rococo style. A distinctive feature is his inclusion of *grotesques*.

Bérain's elaborate ceiling designs often consisted of airy canopies surrounded by springy coils and acanthus foliage, enhanced by graceful figures. The ceilings for royal palaces were even more elaborate. They were adorned with painted allegories and fancy designs. Le Brun's ceiling for the Galerie des Glaces at Versailles is an extraordinary example. The visitor to the palace can follow Louis XIV's life through the ceiling's paintings. On the signing of the Treaty of Nijmegen, the Sun King asked Le Brun to depict his government's triumph on the hall's ceiling. Le Brun designed thirty compositions, framed by stucco work, as a monumental homage to the monarch's military victories in the Dutch Wars of the 1660s and 1670s. For the first time he was portrayed as a person rather than as a mythological figure. This narrative illustrates the move from war to peace. The central painting, *The King Governs for Himself*, 1661, depicts the moment when Louis, after having assumed the throne in 1643 at age four, finally possesses total power. Prior to painting the canvases, Le Brun made hundreds of preparatory drawings. After the canvases were completed, they were attached to the vaulted ceiling.

The Galerie des Glaces has recently been unveiled after a

François Joseph Bélanger's study for the dining room ceiling in the Pavillon de Bagatelle. The Metropolitan Museum of Art, Harris Brisbane Dick Fund, 1932.

three-year restoration, the same amount of time that it took Le Brun to paint the hall's ceilings. During this restoration, scenes that were painted over during previous repairs were discovered underneath. The original vibrant hues used by Le Brun—including a highly precious lapis lazuli pigment unaffected by time—were also revealed. Le Brun's historical narrative of the Sun King's reign, conveyed through symbolism, costumery, and gestures, is a monumental feat. His magnificent ceilings illustrate the glory of French seventeenth-century decoration.

In addition to creating masterful ceilings, Le Brun clearly knew their role and how to integrate them into a room ensemble. He understood that the beauty of a room can only be judged by someone standing inside it who experiences the effects of its scale, harmony of color, architectural elements, and the unity of these parts. Praising Le Brun's ceiling at Vaux-le-Vicomte, Mademoiselle de Scudery sums up his achievement: *Tout ce que l'on voit en ces peintures satisfait également les yeux et la raison.* (It is the ultimate goal to please the eye as well as the mind. This was achieved in those painted ceilings.)

During the eighteenth century, pomp and majesty gave way to charm and elegance, as well as voluptuousness. It was the time of the *petits appartements*. In these smaller rooms, a feeling of coziness was created through elegantly carved ceilings, which were sometimes covered with gilded scrolls. Sometimes monkeys, chinamen, or arabesques, created by such painters as Jean-Antoine Watteau (1684–1721) and Christophe Huet (d. 1759), trail up the walls to the ceiling. One of the best examples of this decorative genre is the Château de Chantilly's *Grande Singerie* in one of the *salons,* which Huet painted in 1735. The main figures in this space are chinamen with their monkey attendants, amiable and perky little creatures who climb all over the

Chic Advice

Even if today's decoration has taken a turn toward greater simplicity, a few pointers from the past are useful. Medallions can be added in the center of a ceiling to accentuate the base of a chandelier. They can also be used as an accent. Cove can be tremendously useful in concealing indirect lighting, and coffered ceilings can give immediate structure to a room. Therefore, knowledge of the grandiose ceilings of the past can be very helpful in understanding architectural tricks.

- Colors also play an important role in ceilings. Nothing creates greater height and depth than a ceiling painted a pale aqua.

- A ceiling covered with mirror can create different atmospheres—from naughtiness to cleanliness. A ceiling of tented fabric suggests an exotic setting while a dark-colored ceiling creates a snug sanctuary. So, a *plafond*, like a floor, contributes to the ambience and mood of a room.

walls and ceiling. Mandarins and monkeys are mixed so freely that it is often difficult to tell the difference between animal and man. They are depicted on door panels, shooting at dragonflies, or languidly resting in hammocks; they scamper around the stucco scrolls on the ceiling. This room is one of the most attractive surviving examples of French Rococo interior decoration, and certainly the most whimsical.

With the advent of Neoclassicism, the decoration of ceilings continued to be complex. Monkeys and scrolls gave way to Greek and Roman motifs. At Bagatelle, François Joseph Bellanger (1744–1818) designed intricate ceilings, enhanced with cameos, antiques, nymphs, and *guirlandes* (garlands) for Louis XVI's younger brother, Comte d'Artois. Elaborate ceilings continued to be an important part of interior decoration. Under the influence of Charles Percier (1764–1838) and Pierre-François Léonard Fontaine (1762–1853), proponents of the Empire style, they evolved once again. For the first time, the term "interior decoration" was used in their *Recueil de Décorations Intérieurs* of 1801 (reissued in 1812). Illustrated in this book were entire rooms in the Empire style outfitted with ceilings decorated with pilasters, *rosaces*, and painted foliages.

Often, the decorative schemes of ceilings had to be completed quickly. Hence, draped ceilings resembling tents became a fashionable alternative. In humbler houses, where the moldings were fairly simple, ceilings were painted a grayish white.

FLOORS

Floors are an important feature of the architectural shell. For centuries wooden floors have been a stylish way to finish a house. Great planks sawed from wide tree trunks were used in simple dwellings, while palaces were decorated with sophisticated inlaid or parquet floors. Wooden floors were primarily made of waxed oak. Over the centuries, they have been painted and enhanced, often to mimic more expensive materials or just to create a pretty pattern.

During the seventeenth century, Versailles was the leading inspiration for not only ceiling decoration but also floors. In 1693, the brilliant Swedish architect, Nicodamus Tessin was very keen to hear about the new decorations of Versailles, as he wished to replicate them in the Royal Palace in Stockholm. The letters between the Swedish diplomat in France Daniel Cronström and Tessin describe how the floors of Versailles's Galerie des Glaces were treated. They should be rubbed, with *un peu de cire jaune de sorte que les bois de chênes à sa couleur naturelle, a cela prêt que la cire le rend un peu plus jaune* (with a little bit of yellow wax so that the natural color of the oak floor will come through, and the wax will just enhance the yellow tone). Tessin was also told that the floors needed to be polished with *une brosse à frotter le parquet*. Three months later, a specimen was sent to him. He was also informed that: *Il y a une frieze ou bande de marbre noir de 8 pouces environ qui régne tout autour des lambris en bas*, while at the Trianon *où il n'y à point de lambris de marbre les parquets touches aux lambris. Il n'y a qu'une seule piece à Versailles dont le parquet soit par quarrés tout le reste est en lozenges à la nouvelle manière.*

(There is a black marble border of about eight thumbs going all around he baseboards but at Trianon none of that exists as the floor goes all the way to the baseboards. There is only one spot at Versailles where the parquet is done the old-fashioned way, in square, and the rest is in the shape of lozenges as this was the new fashion.) Cronström's letters home continue to be invaluable sources of information about design of this time.

Parquet laid diagonally (*en lozenges*) is still called *parquet de Versailles*. The term *parquet* refers to the small, fenced-in park where justice was administered. It was often a raised platform, quite special in order to stress its importance. Parquet was first used in such a context—hence the name. *Parquet* literally means "little park." By the end of the seventeenth century, parquet had been widely adopted for all the principal rooms in important French buildings.

In private rooms reserved for royalty, very elaborate marquetry (inlaid) floors were used, suggesting yet another level of sophistication. Versailles' Dauphin's Closet, known as the *Cabinet Doré*, had an intricate *parquet marquété* designed by Pierre Golé in 1692. In the Grand Cabinet next door, Louis XIV's son, the Dauphin, had a floor executed by the acclaimed André-Charles Boulle. However, floors of such complexity were the exception.

Having a roof over our head and a floor under our feet is one of the basic human comforts. A stable floor creates the base of any construction, and its solidity provides stability both to the structure and its habitants. The sometimes forgotten floor is one of the most crucial features of a room or building. It really can be considered a fifth wall. And, *pourquoi pas?* The floor is, after all, a primary design element and gives a space its flavor. Stones create an old-fashioned feel, carpets a homey atmosphere, and marble a look of luxury. Flooring also works as a great unifier in a home, allowing rooms to be linked seamlessly or set apart in just the right way.

OPPOSITE, CLOCKWISE FROM TOP LEFT: One of the most effective ways of adding decoration to a wooden floor is to use stencils to create repeating motifs.

The painted white wood floor of the pool house is enhanced with a dark green leaf-shaped stencil design, which is repeated in a smaller scale on the table.

The stencil design is handmade and repeated as a frieze around the table of the summer dining room to give the impression of a carpet border.

A larger view of the stenciled floor, integrating both elements: the dainty leaf stencil and the bold geometric border.

Another detail of a stencil in the pool house. This one is a geometric pattern that functions as a border in the main room, separating the leaf stencil and providing a bold contrast.

First and foremost, floor covering should never be considered a cover-up. Keep in mind that a floor must confidently accommodate the demands of constant traffic. This is no small task! While we tend to focus on the aesthetic aspects of flooring, it is essential to factor in the practical.

There have never been so many flooring possibilities as today. Design options continue to proliferate. Time-honored marble, stone, and precious and non-precious woods have already paved the way (no pun intended!) for such modern materials as concrete, glass, cork, rubber, and all sorts of carpeting. So many choices can be very confusing, understandably, for the neophyte. My advice is, when in doubt, use common sense.

As with most things, knowledge is power. Try to educate yourself as thoroughly as possible on the subject of flooring. Figure out what kind of look you are after. Be a realist and keep in mind what kind of household you have and what your traffic patterns are. Dogs and kids will force you to choose something durable that can easily be cleaned. Remember, flooring is a costly investment. Choose a covering that is pleasing to the eye and appropriate to the room. If possible, try to select flooring that will improve with age. *Bonne chance!*

Chic Advice

- One way to create flooring that is both cheap and chic is to follow historical tradition. Polished, oiled, stained, painted, pickled, stenciled, or varnished wooden floorboards have a timeless, classic quality that appeals to many of us, making them suitable for rustic, contemporary, or sophisticated homes.

- Today's products enable you to protect your floor very effectively, without constant waxing or buffing. A change of heart and some sanding and staining will make your floors look new in a flash and at a minimal cost.

Traditional Parquet Floors Parquet floors are laid with square-edged wooden blocks rather than with tongue-and-groove strips. Because parquet is made of solid wood—unlike today's modern veneers or thin tongue-and-groove boards—neglected parquet floors can be brought back to life by sanding and finishing with a suitable, satin seal.

Painted Floors Paint can add a tone of whimsy to your decorating scheme. For me, it is a fabulous solution. Paint works wonders on the most tired woodwork. A single expanse of colors will instantly smarten the rattiest wooden floor. I am personally partial to a soft white. It invariably makes a room look bigger, visually pushing back the walls, setting a cool, calm, clean tone.

The preparation and painting of a wooden floor is straightforward and simple—a great plus in my book. Wash the boards thoroughly with a brush, soap, and water. Let them dry. Apply a coat of primer, then paint and finish with two coats of varnish. Paint is also a perfect way to re-create a complicated marquetry floor.

Another technique to dress up a floor is with stenciling. Use manila cardboard to create floor stencils. They are best applied with a hard brush. Select your general pattern beforehand. Consider a center pattern, a border, or both. When dry, painted floors should be protected by two or three coats of acrylic floor varnish.

OPPOSITE, CLOCKWISE FROM TOP LEFT: Floor covering comes in countless materials.

Different wood stains are used to imitate various wood types. This is a good technique for creating patterns and designs.

The marble floor of the bathroom is dark green with an inset design of white marble, creating a geometric pattern—white on green.

Limestone is always an elegant solution, as seen here in the *jardin d'hiver*. This surface is conducive to radiant heat and easy to maintain with numerous plants atop.

The two-tone parquet floor's striped effect echoes the white-and-black stripes of the zebra rug.

Limed Wood Floors This effect is achieved by rubbing limed paste or wax onto the floor, then sealing the surface with two or more coats of varnish. It is best to use this treatment on an oak floor. The effect is less pronounced on soft woods, such as pine.

Flagstone Floors In past centuries, stone floors were found in great architectural structures as well as in modest dwellings. Surprising but true! Stone was not considered a luxury but rather a ubiquitous building material. Originally, the choice of a stone was confined to what was available locally. Therefore, the interior and exterior of an old building harmonized with the landscape. I still associate French regions with different stone coloring. It is important to consider what kind of stone you want to use. Once again, think of the mantra of suitability.

The most common types of stone used in flagstone flooring design were limestone and sandstone. The benefit of such flooring is that it improves with age. Flagstones retain ambient temperature. In the past they were beloved for their cooling effect; nowadays they are a great medium for radiant heat. Limestone has been traditionally used in the great halls, entrances, and staircases of a château, often with a black keystone inset or by itself. Its pale, natural tone possesses an almost sensual appeal enhanced by the passage of time. Limestone is also about nearly half the cost of marble.

It is imperative to seal limestone and sandstone as they are quite porous. They are best suited for an entrance, stairs, hallways, and bathrooms. Flagstone may not be the best choice for a hard-working kitchen since if you drop a glass on this surface it will surely shatter.

A side view of the pool house. The stones around it are easy on the feet. They also reflect the light and integrate seamlessly with the landscape.

Marble Floors Marble has always been considered the king of flooring materials, often associated with palaces, castles, and churches. The Romans were the first to use marble in slabs, thanks to their invention of cement, which was essential to hold the marble in place. The widespread use of marble began in the first century B.C. in Rome. By the time of Augustus, marble was used everywhere. Marble used for floors in antiquity was colored—red, serpentine green porphyry, white, or *giallo antico* (a yellow ocher). By alternating light and dark marbles, lively patterns with unusual hues were created. Since marble is inherently cool, it is widely used in Mediterranean and other warm countries in order to keep the temperature low indoors.

Traditionally, marble is polished to give it a glossy sheen, which is achieved with varying degrees of abrasive sanding. This helps to give it a resistance to water and therefore makes marble an ideal material for floors. From the middle of the seventeenth century on, numerous French publications display the infinite variations for a marble floor: *echiquier en lozenge, croisée en pointe de diamant, platebande, lozenge tranchés, octagonal et quarré.* C. A. d'Aviler in his *Court d'Architecture*, published in 1738, shows a variety of marble flooring options. A large palette of colors and textures are available: Pink and black marbles are quarried in Portugal, reds and grays in Spain, whites and creams traditionally come from Italy and Greece, while greens are now imported from China and India.

Marble can be fragile and easily stained (especially with grease marks, which are hard to remove) when not properly sealed. These days, excellent sealers have improved resistance to stains and make cleaning easier. Still, be careful with oil, and remember that wine can stain marble forever.

CHIC & COZY CARPETS

The carpet evokes images of fantasy. From exotic tales of magic come the fantastic flying carpet. (Remember *Ali Baba and the Forty Thieves*!) Did you ever have that dream of closing your eyes and sitting on a flying carpet, which would take you in an instant wherever you wished to go? I certainly have many times.

From the *Ballets Russes* sets for *Scheherazade* to countless Hollywood productions, the carpet conjures up an image of luxury and even voluptuousness. It also has a sacred air: Think of the church altar, the carpet under the Virgin's throne, or the throne of a king, and, of course, the Muslim prayer rug. The presence of a carpet can immediately finish a room. It also creates a cozy and exotic atmosphere.

Dating to ancient times, the carpet is Oriental in origin. Words found on Assyrian clay tablets attest to the use of knotted carpets as floor coverings as early as the nineteenth century B.C. We do not know for certain when knotted pile rugs were first produced. Modern scholars consider that the technique originated in Mongolia and was brought to the Middle East with migrating tribes. Ancient writers refer to weaving and its many forms. Al-Khatib in his *History of Baghdad* tells us that the palace of the Abbasid Caliph was decorated with many carpets and fabrics for the reception of the Byzantine ambassadors in 917.

The earliest known knotted pile carpet is a large well-preserved fragment discovered in Siberia dating back to the fifth century B.C. There is documentation to suggest that pile knotting was established in Persia and Turkey by the beginning of the Christian era. With the rise and spread of Islam from the seventeenth century, carpet weaving began to be documented by Arabic-speaking poets and writers. In fact, in very old carpets the date is often woven into the design. Techniques such

as crochet, needlepoint, embroidery, or knitting are also used to create rugs. These types of rugs were developed later on and have succumbed to the overwhelming popularity of pile carpets.

The influx of foreigners throughout Europe led to fresh interpretations of the pile carpet. This was largely due to the presence of the Moors in Spain, the Crusades of the eleventh to the thirteenth centuries, the travels of Marco Polo in the late thirteenth century, and the Venetians' voyages to the East from the thirteenth century. This cross-fertilization is responsible for creative carpet designs. A carpet's function was not limited to the floor. Carpets were also used as table coverings and altar cloths. In fact, from the mid-fourteenth century on, Oriental carpets frequently appear in European genre and biblical paintings. Among the latter, Venetian artist Francesco Bassano the Elder's (c. 1475–1539) *Virgin and Child Enthroned,* 1519, shows a keyhole carpet under the Madonna's feet, and Nicolas Tournier's (1590–1639) painting, *The Concert,* c. 1630–35, shows a large Ushak draped over the table. The oldest European pile rugs were produced in Spain. It was here that the Moorish influence was the most pronounced. Following the expulsion of the Moors from Spain in the sixteenth century, the quality of Spanish rugs declined.

In Europe, for the first time, carpets became an integral component of a decorating scheme. They were given equal prominence with furniture design and interior decorations.

At the beginning of the seventeenth century in France, Pierre Dupont opened a workshop at the Louvre to make carpets in the Oriental manner. However, in

French carpet rendering, c. 1852, part of a series that hangs in my entrance hall.

1627 he founded another one in a former soap factory. The name *savonnerie* was applied to the carpets that were produced there. Savonnerie carpets were of the highest quality and thoroughly European in design, with acanthus scrolls and classical emblems. This workshop flourished during the early part of Louis XIV's reign. Its most important commission was for the magnificent carpets for the Galerie d'Apollon and Grande Galerie in the Louvre. The latter were never used. Woven between 1664 and 1683, these nearly one hundred carpets reflect the fashion of this period—richly patterned with Baroque acanthus scrolls against backgrounds of deep and noble reds, browns, and blacks. Savonnerie carpets were so refined that they were reserved exclusively for royalty. After 1805 the workshop was employed by Napoleon I to produce carpets in the Empire style. Savonnerie carpet production became so successful that a tapestry workshop was added. It led to the creation of the famed Gobelins factory. Tapestry and carpets had thus become related.

Competition arose in the mid-eighteenth century with the introduction of simpler designs that were aimed at the prosperous bourgeoisie. Aubusson had become a rival workshop. Aubusson carpets, with their thick-knotted piles, were made on vertical looms. Using the tapestry technique, short-pile carpets were woven on horizontal looms. These carpet designs consisted of symmetrical patterns that incorporated classical motifs. The Huguenots had to flee France after Louis XIV revoked the Edict of Nantes in 1685; many were artisans from the Aubusson and the Savonnerie workshops. A weaving industry was soon born in England.

Later, during the nineteenth century, there was an influx of individual workshops dedicated to creating rug designs in many different styles, including Arts and Crafts, Art Nouveau, Neo-Gothic, and Art Deco.

The advent of the Industrial Revolution drastically altered the course of carpet production. Carpets became easier and cheaper to make. The revolutionary *moquette* (wall-to-wall carpeting) was developed by Alexander Smith & Son of Yonkers, New York. The era of ultimate luxury had finally arrived only a couple of hundred years after Savonnerie and Aubusson carpets originated in France.

OPPOSITE, CLOCKWISE FROM TOP LEFT:
The needlepoint Stark rug, surrounding the sofas in the pool house, gives the room a cozy feeling and stands in contrast to the clean simple statement of the white stenciled floor.

A modern variation of a rug. Warm and cozy, a soft and sensual carpet is the most indulgent of all floor covering.

The wool sisal carpet with its light caramel color and brilliant wide orange border brightens the library. This room is quite large so the border pulls the space together instead of constricting it.

A dramatic sweep of carpet transforms stairs into an elegant climb. Stair carpets receive the most abuse of all flooring in a house, so choose wisely. This cheetah-patterned runner is deceptively resistant. It is used throughout the house, creating a unifying effect. Orange piping adds a final chic touch.

Chic Advice

Today, carpets, contemporary or antique, are still a major investment. There are so many styles to choose from that the only way to narrow it down is through personal taste. Carpets can define the look of a space, so select wisely and then treat them with care.

Care

Try to keep your carpets as clean as possible since grime, dirt, and stains can destroy even the heaviest pile if they are left unclean long enough. To clean small area rugs, an old-fashioned carpet beater is considered the best tool for the job. Carpet beaters are still made in the Middle East and are available in some houseware stores.

◆ Carpet beating is a perfect way to work out your aggressions! Choose a dry day when there is no wind. Wear old clothes. After hanging the carpet on an outdoor clothesline, beat it from the back. (It is very important to beat it from the back to avoid driving the dust back into the knots.) It's amazing how much dust can be stored in an old carpet. Oriental rugs can be beaten hard. Be gentle with needlepoint and hooked rugs. After beating, vacuum the rug. Use the curtain-cleaning attachment of the vacuum hose. For fragile area rugs that cannot be taken outside, spread out an old sheet or a thick layer of brown paper and lay the rug on it. Do not use newspaper, as the ink may stain the carpet. Hit the back gently with the beater, shaking the whole rug from time to time to let the dirt fall out onto the paper. Then vacuum the back carefully.

◆ Never let an area rug hang outside overnight. Dew or sudden showers will dampen the fabric and it will take days to dry out; in addition, it will smell bad.

◆ To store rugs, keep them flat and wrapped in brown paper. Never store rugs in plastic. Rugs too big to lie flat can be rolled around a light pole, with the pile inside. Hooked rugs should be rolled with the pile on the outside.

A French needlepoint carpet, nineteenth century, next to a Kilim-upholstered chair.

Colors & Walls

Parfums, couleurs et sons se font echos.

(Perfumes, colors, and sounds echo one another.)

—Charles Baudelaire (1821–67)

COLORS

Colors are for me one of the most potent elements in a decorative scheme—and the least expensive, by the way. Just change the shade of your walls from white to bright red and the room will assume a new lease on life. You do not need to be that radical in order to achieve stunning results.

First, it is important to understand the meaning of colors because an individual's response to colors is more emotional than rational. There is definitely a psychological language at work here. For example, psychologists have reported that children tested in brightly colored rooms had higher scores than those tested in rooms with bland colors. It is a common misconception that our ancestors did not like bright colors. Through the centuries, age, dirt, and dust have dulled the brightness of many of the vivid shades used centuries ago. After careful restoration and study, many art historians can attest to the intensity of colors used in the past, from Roman town houses to eighteenth-century châteaux. At the end of the seventeenth century, Sir Isaac Newton, experimenting with sunlight refracted through a prism, made some important discoveries concerning color. To illustrate his findings, he arranged the color spectrum into a wheel. White, like its counter-color black, is at the extreme end of the spectrum with blue falling in between green and violet.

White (*blanc*). White is absolute, meaning either a total lack of color or the sum of all colors. Therefore, it represents the beginning as well as the end of life. The symbols associated with white reflect both the color's philosophical and cultural meanings. In the Christian religion, angels are always depicted in white, as is the representation of ghosts. Hence the saying, "white as a ghost." For all these reasons, white originally was the color of death and mourning. It was the color of mourning at the French court for many centuries, and it remains so today in the Orient. The French queen Marie Antoinette adored white and only wore white linen dresses in her fanciful Hameau de Trianon. As we know, white is also the symbol of purity, and is therefore linked to the notion of a new beginning. This is why the new bride traditionally wears a virginal white dress.

Lighter colors immediately lift the spirit of a room. The southern exposure is perfect for this citrus green summer dining room wall. A darker shade is better for a room with a northern exposure. Do not be afraid of color—it is one of the most effective ways of decorating a space.

Blue (*bleu*). Blue is the coolest of all colors, with true blue the deepest. The eye can lose itself in blue's seeming otherworldliness. For the painter Wassily Kandinsky, a master of colors, blue has *une gravité solennelle, supra terrestre* (a gravity reminiscent of death). It is why the walls of the pyramids in ancient Egypt were always painted a shade of blue. The color of the House of France was *Bleu Royal* and its crest was *d'azur aux trois fleurs de lys d'or*, anchoring the supra-terrestrial power of this Catholic ruler. Louis XIV's famous portrait, painted by Hyacinthe Rigaud in 1701, showed the monarch in all his regalia swathed in a gigantic blue velvet coat embellished with gold *fleurs de lys*, emblems of his absolute power. A blue setting is peaceful and relaxing, but unlike green, is totally devoid of tonality. For some people (like me, for example) blue, because of its ethereal quality, can be depressing. This negative association is illustrated in the popular language: for example, *avoir une peur bleue* (to be very frightened) or *Il n'y vois que du bleu* (he hasn't seen anything). Pale blue is refreshing, almost neutral—an invitation to dream.

Green (*vert*). As described by Kandisky, green gives an impression of *repos terrestre et de contentement de soi* (peace on earth and happiness with oneself). It is the color of hope and strength. *Pas mal!* No wonder I am so found of this color! However, green has its two sides. The emerald that is a papal color is also the sign of Lucifer before his fall. Green can possess *un pouvoir maléfique* (evil power), like all female symbols. Green is a female color (red is male). Vincent van Gogh, another master of color, understood this perfectly. In a letter of September 8, 1888, he wrote to his brother Theo: *J'ai cherché à exprimer avec le rouge et le vert les terribles passions humaines.* (I have tried with red and green to express violent human passions.) Green has a powerful, complicated character stemming from its dichotomy: the green of spring brings hope, while the green of decay signals death. Studies show that green is the most peaceful color if it is quite pale.

Red (*rouge*). Red historically has been associated with anger, violence, and blood. (What else can be expected from a male?) It is universally recognized as a symbol of life itself. The red in the Revolutionary flag propelled men and women to action. The red lamp standing outside the whorehouse was intended to stimulate the libido, and therefore arouse it, too. Dark red was the color *par excellence* of power in ancient Rome—the color of the emperors. Justinian's code even condemned to death anyone caught buying or selling red cloth.

Purple (*violet*). In between red and blue is the divine purple. The color of patience and temperance, purple became the color of the princes of the Church—*évèques* (bishops) and *archévèques* (archbishops). It also represents the passage to death and was often a color associated with some form of mourning. The poet Rimbaud understood the melancholic tone associated with violet: "*O. Omega, rayon violet de tes yeux.*"

Various paint treatments create texture and interest. This fireplace has acquired an extra dimension as a result of the faux-marble finish.

The paint used on this wall is a special color, a shade of lavender; the texture, a mixture of sponging and marbleizing, enhances the color and adds depth. The semi-gloss white painted chair rail makes the color pop even more.

Yellow (*jaune*). Yellow is rarely mellow, probably the warmest of all colors, representing light and life. Kandinsky describes yellow as: *Le jaune a une telle tendance au clair qu'il ne peut y avoir de jaune trés foncé. On peut donc dire qu'il existe une affinité profonde, physique entre le jaune et le blanc.* (Yellow has a tendency to be light; therefore it is impossible to have a very dark shade of yellow. The conclusion is that there is a deep, physical connection between yellow and white.) The paler shade of *jaune* is associated with cowardice. Darker yellow means wisdom and is the color of eternity, just as gold is the metal of eternity.

Different civilizations prefer different colors. Color preferences are linked to the varying intensity of the sun in a particular country as well as cultural traditions. So, Northern Europeans are thought to prefer subdued shades, and bright, strong colors are favored in the Mediterranean region.

Prior to the chemical discovery of "mauveine" in England in 1856 by a young boy (later known as Sir William Perkins) all colors and pigments had to be extracted from natural materials. *Rubia tinctorum* was the standard source of reds, and thousands of tons of the plant had to be carted to every textile town. This was not very practical. Indigo, which the Romans obtained from shellfish for their "imperial purple," was the main source of blues. Fustic or annatto gave yellow. Some shades and colors, notably greens, could only be achieved by double dyeing. The range was as infinite as it is today, although the process was just a bit slower.

If used properly, color can be a formidable creative tool. Personally, I adore colors for their infinite variety and possibilities for combination. In eighteenth-century France the dominant colors on the walls were delicate pastels, often enhanced with white and sometimes gold as a way to express luxury and leisure, and show a total disdain for practical consideration—*le comble du chic*.

It is important to remember that colors are grouped into families. A single color includes its lighter and darker versions, which are called a hue. Any hue that is mixed with gray or black to darken it is known as a shade. The dullness or brightness of a color or its concentration of pure pigment is called chroma or intensity. The simplest and most familiar color theory is based on the concept that there are three primary colors: red, blue, and yellow, and three secondary colors: green, orange, and violet. Secondary colors are obtained by mixing equal parts of two primary colors together. Then there are the six intermediate colors. The easiest way to look at them is on a color wheel, available at any local hardware store. Each hue has its own "temperature," which affects people and houses in different ways. For example, red and yellow are warm and invigorating, and they tend to blend together whatever is against them. Red and yellow are known as advancing colors because they actually give the impression of being nearer to us. In reality, this phenomenon leads us to two seemingly paradoxical results: If you upholstered your sofa in an intense red, its size will appear to increase, but if you paint the wall of a room a deep red, it will decrease in its apparent spaciousness because the wall will seem closer. The reverse happens with blue, green, and violet. In their various hues, these colors tend to appear cool and restful, giving the impression that they are farther away than they actually are. For precisely that reason they are called receding hues. Used on furniture, they characteristically reduce the apparent size of the object, but when applied to walls they seem to increase a room's dimensions.

Chic Advice

Light colors are used to introduce a feeling of space and airiness into a room. Rather than stop the eye, they appear to let it look beyond and through the space. In essence, light colors recede and give the feeling of pushing the walls out. They usually take full advantage of the natural light and can be used to make artificial light more effective. For example, when a ceiling is painted white or a pale color (light blue is a great alternative), it appears higher than it really is. Similarly, white underfoot visually expands the floor space. Bright strong colors tend to diminish the size of a room. However, my advice is that if a room is small and dark, do not fight it. It is much better to accentuate its weakness and paint the walls a strong, bold color; the effect in the room will be warm and cozy. Closely blended colors are another effective trick. They will conceal or hide architectural defects. An eyesore radiator or air-conditioning unit can become virtually invisible when painted the same color as the walls.

- As a rule, always select a fabric or a paint sample both in the daylight and also at night, under artificial light. It's important to remember that the shade will appear slightly different in each instance.

- Natural light coming from a northern exposure is a cold light and accentuates blue and violet. Natural light with direct sunlight from south or west is a warm light that intensifies yellow, red, and orange, and neutralizes blue and violet. Flourescent light is a real killer for colors because it creates a bluish washed-out look.

- When you are ready to select a new interior color, remember the golden rule: Colors change with light. And above all, simplification is key. Use a few select colors that enhance a space and speak to you. That's real style.

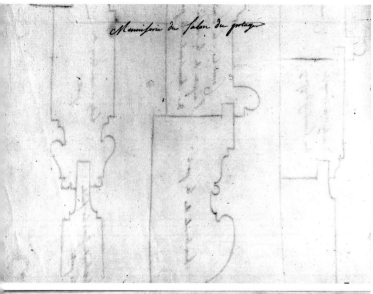

WALLS

Walls in the past have been regarded as surfaces to be decorated—with paintings, murals, panels, tapestry, wallpaper, and moldings—in order to either warm up a room or dress it up.

Wood paneling was originally an elegant means of insulation. The best work was custom-made for the room, with intricate moldings, overmantels, and door panels, and decorative framing for the windows and doors. The two principal timbers used for paneling in France in the seventeenth century were pine and oak. Both were usually painted, although in a few fashionable *hôtels particuliers* at the end of the century, one might find rooms *boisées à la capucine*, which was a term used to described varnished oak paneling because it seemed as dry as the walls of the cell of a Capuchin monk. The monotony of wood was avoided by sophisticated carving and by painting it. It is probably the reason that painted panels were so fashionable and popular. Carvings on paneling were for the most part confined to the surrounding moldings, while the field remained plain and therefore lent itself well to various painted motifs such as landscapes, portraits, and

TOP: The addition of intricate moldings and carvings helps to avoid monotony in walls. This drawing shows a detailed example of cornices at La Quintinie, the house of the *grand jardinier* at Versailles, built in 1682. The drawing bears the inscription: *Menuiserie du salon du potager*. National Museum, Stockolm. Collection Tessin-Härleman.

CENTER: Design for a wood-panel wall decoration with chimneypiece, doorways, and parallel frames, by Antoine Le Pautre (1621–79). The Metropolitan Museum of Art, Rogers Fund, 1961.

BOTTOM: Design for the architectural decoration of the wall of a room with military and naval trophies, late eighteenth century. Wall enhancement came in all forms and shapes to fit the place and its inhabitants. The Metropolitan Museum of Art, Rogers Fund, 1965.

OPPOSITE: Two framed graphic late eighteenth-century French carpet renderings play off the wall's height and infuse the aqua walls with a touch of color.

chinoiserie, as well as lacquer finishes. Another way to dress up wood paneling was through wood graining—the painted imitation of a timber, often a rare one or several mixed together in a pattern, usually executed on "deal" paneling, which was relatively inexpensive, and is similar to our plywood today.

Closely related to graining, and equally popular in the seventeenth century, is marbling, and this was often mixed together. However, Tessin once again inform us of the latest craze in Paris in 1693: *On ne peint les chambres boisées, les portes, les volets, les chassis, les plafonds, les portes, que de blanc avec le filet d'or où sans or.* (One no longer paints paneled rooms, shutters, window-frames, ceilings, and doors anything but white with or without narrow gilded moldings.)

What is interesting is that the fad of white-paneled rooms, enhanced with gold, continued well into the next century along with pale *rechampie* combinations—moldings painted two or three different tones, such as yellow and blue or blue and pink. Today, as a variation on the historical usage, it is a nice idea to have wood paneling, and even wainscoting, painted a different color than the walls. Painting your walls is a perfect option, too, one which has been done for centuries, providing that the plaster or sheet rock is in decent condition. Wavy or cracked walls are not the most aesthetically pleasing look. Imagine how tricky it would be to hang paintings or even mirrors on such walls! A funny anecdote: When Tessin was at Versailles in 1687, he noted that the pictures in the Dauphin's Closet were protected by blinds of painted satin on rollers, fitted with a spring that held the blinds down in front of the pictures. Imagine, we could start a new trend, and follow on the Dauphin's footsteps, putting blinds on paintings.

Hanging paintings and mirrors are effective decorative features in a room. Either organize large groupings or single out one particularly special canvas. In the seventeenth century, and even the eighteenth, most people did not hang their pictures in a particularly organized manner. The hanging height seemed to be different from today; it was much higher. This was probably because paintings were not hung flat against the wall. They were mostly canted forward. Mirrors or looking glasses became very popular and were often mixed with paintings on a wall. When you think of it, things have not changed all that much. *Plus ça change, et plus c'est la même chose.*

Colors and wall decorations work hand in hand. The various color and paint techniques enhance the architectural details. The faux-marble finish gives extra weight to the niche, while the deep green reinforces its shape, and the turquoise line detail makes the juxtaposition of colors more interesting.

Chic Advice

Walls are the display case—or *écrin*—of a room. Treat them well and with care. Skim coat their outer layer, if necessary, adorn and embellish them with crown moldings, a baseboard, windows, and a door frame, and they will pay you back in spades. Then if you run out of ideas or effects, you can always try *trompe l'oeil*; it hides a multiplicity of sins. *Vive la peinture!*

Danger often comes from unexpected places: Wallpaper can be deadly. Oscar Wilde (1854–1900) made this unfortunate discovery on his deathbed in 1900, prompting the comment, *My wallpaper is killing me— one of us must go.*

An extreme case to be sure; fortunately wallpaper rarely has had such a negative effect on most people. On the contrary, wallpaper properly planned and designed has a powerful cosmetic and decorative impact on a room. It gives a fine finished look and dictates a mood more effectively than any other element in furnishings—rich and luxurious, pretty and peaceful, playful and colorful, strong and bold, and even educational in some instances.

The history of wallpaper stretches back further than most people realize and is a subject that is less researched than most other aspects of decorative art. In part due to the fragility and elusiveness of the medium itself, paper, which rots when exposed to humidity and often gets covered and recovered, makes its conservation, not to mention its display, rather difficult for museums.

Wallpaper (like paper itself) is believed to be a Chinese invention. Early historians found that Chinese walls were often lined with wood and handmade paper, sometimes crudely decorated and coated with lacquer, as early as 200 A.D. Paper designs were also produced very early for funeral rites, and copies of them were hung on walls. For special festive occasions, scrolls of either silk or paper were hung on the walls of Chinese houses. They were entirely temporary and changed frequently. Nonetheless they had a strong decorative quality, and a large repertoire soon extended to include flowers, animals, and landscapes.

In Europe, as in China, painted paper decorations preceded printed ones. Also, as in China, they were purely temporary and were often, at the beginning (around the fifteenth century), decorated with biblical designs. This all changed when marble paper appeared with a technique imported from—where else?—Persia. Theses marble papers were undoubtedly used all over Europe as wallpaper—a fashion that survives today. Wallpapers thus became in France and England an inexpensive substitute for tapestry, painted cloth, or leather hangings. Links between wallpaper and printed textiles still exist in much the same form today. Designs are shared by both products, sometimes with the idea that they should be used together in a room with an integrated design, and sometimes with the idea that the same blocks can be utilized as a matter of economic expediency.

The earliest surviving examples date back to the sixteenth century, and it appears that by then wallpaper was in fairly wide use. Those examples were printed from wood blocks with heraldic devices and floral patterns in black on a white ground. A century later, colors were

OPPOSITE, CLOCKWISE FROM TOP LEFT: Wallpaper is an easy way of making a room more attractive. Other architectural effects can be created by adding a wood panel to the lower half of the wall or applying chair-rail molding. This is advisable only if your ceiling height is greater than eight feet; if it is less, the result will not be successful.

Wallpaper with a busy pattern in a bathroom works well because the lower panel of the wall is painted white and creates a clean contrast. The wallpaper theme with coral branches is fitting for a pool house. The coral print pushes the point further, making the decoration coral on coral—a bit of a *clin d'oeil* (a wink).

Wallpaper comes in a multiplicity of shapes and designs, perfect for bathrooms and bedrooms. The large scale of these cheerful tents is a lovely enhancement for a bedroom.

The Pierre Deux toile wallpaper makes this relatively large bedroom feel cozy. This is one of the great attributes of toile and why it is so popular for bedrooms. The design is peaceful and calming, creating a safe haven. Oddly enough, the wallpaper and fabric for the headboard and curtains come from different companies and yet they go well together.

added to wallpaper with the help of stencils. The discovery of flocked paper was yet another brilliant addition to early wallpaper. Flocked paper is embossed, which allows a greater variety of effects to be produced. Its inspiration, too, came from leather hangings, which, painted with gold or silver foil, are often known as Cordova leather. Paper, obviously, was a more economical alternative.

The standard of living in the Western world continued to increase for a larger segment of the population and more emphasis was placed on the home. This manifested itself in many ways, including fashion for wallpapers, which continued to expand through the years. A desire for novelty prompted the creation of new patterns. Flowered and chinoiserie patterns (the continuing attraction of the exotic!) became very popular and as a result, hand-painted Chinese wallpaper was imported in quantity. This was a big boost to the acceptance of wallpaper. The wallpaper business started booming and several firms led the ever-expanding market.

In late eighteenth-century France (despite the Revolution, before, during, and after), the firm Revillon emerged as

the outstanding manufacturer of wallpaper. The next development (still in fashion today) was the introduction of scenic wallpaper by Zuber and Dufour. By the nineteenth century, wallpaper was everywhere, too often in garish combinations. (hence, the Oscar Wilde comment) Some houses appeared to be held together by the wallpaper! Today the fashion for wallpaper still abounds, but in a more balanced manner than in the nineteenth century. The rule of thumb is that not every room benefits from its addition.

Chic Advice

For me, wallpaper is used best in hallways—especially if the space is small—and bathrooms. Small hallways also benefit from a dado (or chair rail), an inexpensive way to create structure and visual interest.

Wallpaper can also be very pretty in bedrooms, especially when used together with a similar or coordinated fabric for curtains or bedcovers. In the case of Chinese wallpaper or a scenic motif, it is most fetching today in a dining room. It can also look very dramatic in an entrance, providing that the space is large enough. I would steer clear of very busy patterns and jarring colors, as they will become overwhelming rather quickly.

The choices are quite limitless, as are the materials, but as in many things, however, editing is important and not overdoing a good thing is best.

Wallpaper Removal
A likely place to find very old wallpaper is under woodwork, which has been added at a later date to an older building. Record everything you find before tampering with it. Old wallpaper is brittle, so proceed carefully. Old glue loses much of its adhesive powers, so with a flat-bladed knife and a lot of patience you can achieve good results.

◆ The bottom paper can frequently be eased off in large sheets by inserting a knife between the plaster and the paper.

◆ Do not roll old wallpaper; it will crack. Keep it flat.

◆ Small fragments can be treated like drawings and should be mounted on a frame between cardboard.

◆ If you have a "paper sandwich" (many layers stuck together), steam them apart.

Old-fashioned wallpaper gives a homey feeling to this guestroom. The old-world quality is further enhanced with a chair rail. The chair-rail molding running all around the room is an added architectural detail. This is another example of how cornices and moldings are used to reinforce the decorative scheme and vice-versa.

Doors & Windows, Curtains & Shades

Give me your tired, your poor,
Your huddled masses yearning to breathe free,
The wretched refuse of your teeming shore,
Send these, the homeless, tempest-tossed, to me:
I lift my lamp beside the golden door.

—Emma Lazarus (1849–87), *The New Colossus,* inscription
for The Statue of Liberty, New York Harbor

DOORS

Right from the beginning, for security reasons doors (*portes*) had to be small, with only a single leaf (*vantail*)—which was often reinforced with nails, metal, or extra pieces of wood—allowing one person at a time to get through. These early doors opened only from the inside. They were reinforced with heavy keys and strong locks. For extra security, they even had in front of them an exterior door with a peephole (*judas*) and small gates. Like windows, doors grew wider and larger as society became more stable.

Castles, royal or not, started to see larger doors, even double doors, from the sixteenth century on. Soon protocol directed that doors of the *salons* in royal houses to be opened on both sides (*à deux vantaux*) as a sign of respect for the king and the princes of royal blood. And of course, doors continued to be lavishly decorated with sculpture, carving, and gilding, as we can observe at the Château de Chambord in the Loire Valley or at the Château d'Anet. Such sumptuous decoration seemed for many to be a waste of time and money because the medieval habit of covering doors with curtains in order to minimize drafts continued for some time. And who would blame them? It must have been horrendously cold in those drafty castles, devoid of central heating and modern amenities such as hot running water. It is understandable that one would try to stay warm. If curtains in front of doors were of help, so be it! Such a habit prompted Philibert de L'Orme to say:

Ayant à y faire ornements, moulures ou cornices, je n'en serai point d'avis, ce serait argent perdu, car lesdits ornements ne se voient, à cause de la

Nineteenth-century front doors often had glass pane panels to let light inside. Delicate lead designs generally reinforced the panes and also created additional architectural interest. As security became less of an issue than in earlier times, the proportions of doors become wider.

81

Menuiserie du salon du potager

ABOVE: Ink drawing of the house of La Quentinie, Louis XIV's head gardener (*jardinier*). Built in 1682 near the vegetable garden of Versailles, the house has a rounded oval transom above the French doors. This remarkable feature can be admired in houses in France and America well into the nineteenth century. National Museum, Stockholm. Tessin-Härleman Collection.

OPPOSITE: The nineteenth-century fan-shaped transom above a glass mirror door is similar to French designed doors of the eighteenth century.

tapisserie qui est toujours devant une porte. (To put ornaments, moldings, or cornices on a door is in my view a waste of money considering that none would be seen with a curtain always in front of it.)

The tradition of having curtains in front of doors (*portières*) in the winter continued especially because, starting in the mid-seventeenth century, classical architects, inspired by Louis XIV, designed most châteaux with double doors *en enfilade*. The architectural effect is dazzling when all the doors are open and you can see the perspective from room to room. However, during the winter months it can be cold. It pushed Madame de Maintenon, the Sun King's mistress, to utter theses words of complaint: *Avec le Roi, il n'y a que grandeur, magnificence et symetrie. Il vaut mieux essuyer tous les vents coulis des portes, afin qu'elles soient vis-à-vis les unes des autres.* (With the king there is only power, magnificence, and symmetry. It does not matter that all the wind comes in as long as the doors are *en enfilade*.) The double doors endured and now we can celebrate their symmetry, craftsmanship, and beauty, safely protected from drafts by modern-day heating. *Ouvrez les portes— que la fête commence!*

Chic Advice

Doors should function as a traffic pattern director. They are an essential element for creating private areas, shutting off noisy children or rambunctious dogs, or dampening burnt odors from the kitchen.

- Do not create an entrance door so small that you cannot get furniture through it. This is a commonly made mistake.

- Make sure to put hinges on the intended side of the door. Obviously your door should not bump into a wall or a piece of furniture.

- Avoid large modern glass doors, which can be a real safety hazard.

- Do not use "French doors" in the front facade. They always belong at the back of the house.

This glass door has small pane glass panels separated by wood. Such a door, inspired by French eighteenth-century examples, provides character to an interior space. The *enfilade*—which you can see through several rooms—follows the classical eighteenth-century architectural plan.

WINDOWS

Windows (*fenêtres*) are openings in a wall that let light, and possibly air, into the room. They can be a mixed blessing, depending on the weather. Windows are a crucial component of a facade, as well as an important element of the interior decoration. Their size and the amount of light they bring inside affect the way the interior looks in more ways than one.

Primitive windows were just holes. The people who lived in those early buildings were in constant darkness. The medieval period was a tumultuous time and security was of the foremost importance. As society became more stable, window size increased.

At first, windows were covered with animal hides or membranes. The diaphragms of cattle were apparently the best for this purpose. Oiled cloth and oiled paper, strengthened by two wires fixed diagonally from opposite corners of the frame, were used, or sometimes even lattices made of wood. It was still hard to look out the window. Soon the question of how light falls in a room became of paramount importance. There is good evidence that architects gave a great deal of thought to natural light as they gradually tried to increase the size of the windows.

In 1551, King Henri II organized the creation of a glass factory at Saint-Germain-en-Laye, led by Tesco Mutio, an Italian. Shortly after, mullioned-glass windows (in which many small pieces of glass are joined together with leading) appeared. By 1600, houses of any pretensions had glazed windows. But glass was still quite expensive and could only be obtained in relatively small pieces. The lattice windows, which only required small "quarries" of glass, remained popular until larger panels became more freely available and less expensive. The openings of windows with leaded glass always posed problems because the panes had to be very small and were fragile. These pieces of glass were also very irregular, quite opaque (often a shade of purple due to manganese deposits), and were full of bubbles. As early as 1624, in his *Architecture Française des*

OPPOSITE: Plants in front of an uncovered window benefit from the natural light and echo the plantings outside the house.

ABOVE: Windows are a vital architectural component of a room as well as of the facade. Their proportion is equally important both inside and outside. Placement determines the way light falls into a room. An unsightly window can be hidden by curtains. Unfortunately it is harder to cover up a window on the exterior—perhaps the only solution is creating a mask of vines.

Bon pour les
deux trumeaux
du cabinet
l'Enhaut

Bastimens Particuliers, Louis Savot included a section dedicated to glass, mentioning that glass made in Normandy was of better quality than that from Lorraine. The former was sold in baskets each containing twenty-four pieces of blown glass, about seventy centimeters in diameter.

Madame de Rambouillet has been credited with introducing the tall "French window," which reached down to the floor, pronouncing: *Fenêtres sans appui, qui règnent de haut en bas, depuis son plat-fond jusqu'à son parterre, rend la pièce très gaie et permet de jouir sans obstacle de l'air, de la vue et du plaisir du jardin.* (These windows without sills, which extend from top to bottom, from the ceiling to the ground, make a room extremely cheerful and permit one to enjoy without hindrance the air, the view, and the pleasure of the garden.) Being able to see outside so clearly was a real novelty.

Pierre Le Muet (1551–1669) in *Traictes Divers* of 1646 explains how to calculate the proportion of these very popular windows. Beginning at the end of the seventeenth century, the most sumptuous *hôtels particuliers* were equipped in their reception rooms with these fashionable *fenêtres à la française*. Such windows were usually finished inside in the manner of *boiseries* (woodwork) and outside with the same color of the stones of the facade, rather than a pure white. The small glass panes were separated and held together by thin wood moldings, as is still done today. Double-pane windows existed in order to create protection against the cold. In 1687, the Orangerie de Versailles had windows of this kind—mercifully—for the protection of the beloved orange trees.

The French term for any window frame is *chassis*, from which the English word "sash" is derived. The French word for "sash window" is *fenêtre à chassis à coulisse*. Luckily, being such a mouthful, such windows were never very popular in France.

Early on, windows had interior shutters, bearing the lovely name of *guichet brisée* or *volets à feuilles*. The shutters not only functioned as a layer of security at night but also helped diminish the sun's rays and protected against the cold. The earliest shutters consisted of a single leaf swinging on hinges on one side. However, being quite a hazard, this form of shutter quickly had to be altered. More compact versions soon appeared, which had two shutters swinging from each side. The shutters were made even more practical by having each leaf arranged so that it could be folded back and then folded away into the recess of the thickness of the window reveal. *Vive le progrès!* Outside shutters (*contrevents* or *persiennes)* made their appearance around 1750 at Versailles in the *appartements* of Mesdames (Louis XV's daughters) and at Compiègne around 1755. These shutters were always painted white, probably to fade into the facade. Shutters were especially useful in the south of France, where they offered some relief from the heat.

Modern windows, such as large picture windows, became possible only after the industrial

OPPOSITE: Ink drawing of French doors, by the *Dessinateur des Bâtiments* du Roi, probably for the Grand Trianon at Versailles in the mid-eighteenth century. These stylish French doors with small pane glass have endured throughout the centuries. This is a look still appreciated today. National Museum, Stockholm.

LEFT: Ink drawing of interior shutters, by the *Dessinateur des Bâtiments* du Roi, probably for the Grand Trianon at Versailles in the mid-eighteenth century. The fashion of such inside shutters started at Versailles around 1750 in the *appartements* of Louis XV's daughters. National Museum, Stockholm.

glass-making process was perfected. Modern windows come in many styles. The choices vary to reflect historical traditions or contemporary design. They are also dictated by the prevailing weather conditions of a particular geographic location. Modern windows are usually glazed with one large sheet of glass per sash, while their predecessors were glazed, as we have seen, with multiple panes. Today, glazing bars (*muntins*) tend to be decorative, generally done in a pattern dictated by the architectural needs of the project.

Windows and doors have a political and social importance as well. Defenestration, for example, which is the act of throwing someone out of a window, took a political significance. The word comes from the Latin "*de*" (out of) and "*fenestra*" (window). The ultimate way of getting rid of a political rival was to defenestrate him.

A tax on windows and doors was created under the Directoire in 1798; it was part of the new social order that stemmed from the Revolution. These were progressive taxes depending on the size and, of course, the wealth of the building. It was also easy to check. Such a tax created a huge opposition; people even decided to eliminate some doors or windows from their facade in order to diminish this insane tax. A Mister Huguet, a member of Parliament, exhibited his outrage in a passionate and poetical speech: *Ne pourrait-on trouver un impôt moins rebutant et moins odieux? Quoi! Si pour adorer la divinité, au lieu du soleil, je veux ouvrir une fenêtre à l'Orient, il faudra payer un impôt!* (Couldn't one find less a tax less shocking and less odious? What! If to adore the divinity, instead of the sun, I want to open a window onto the Orient, it will be necessary to pay a tax!)

Chic Advice

- ◆ Avoid too large picture windows as they are not very chic.

- ◆ Make sure the windows are not wider than their height and that there are not too many or too few openings. Remember, we are no longer in the Middle Ages! You do not want to distort the look of the facade.

- ◆ Try to avoid installing skylights. They are too often a source of problems such as water leakage.

- ◆ To protect furniture, paintings, or fabric in a room, install readily available UV filters on the windows.

The *jardin d'hiver* features tall French windows, which extend to the floor. This type of window was introduced by Madame de Rambouillet in the seventeenth century.

CURTAINS & SHADES

In the winter, more than any other time of the year, it is important to feel comfortable in your home. By six o'clock it is pitch dark, and in order to protect your privacy, or just to give yourself the feeling that the dampness of the night will not reach you, it is nice to be able to close the curtains or the shades. With that simple gesture, all of a sudden the world seems to be kept at bay, and the room immediately feels cozier, cut off from outside intrusions, protected by its impregnable soft barrier. What a miracle! That simple everyday movement allows you to create in a second a heaven for yourself. It also demonstrates the powerful psychological power of decorating, with a strong partition made of soft fabric.

Curtains (*rideaux*) demonstrate the powerful decorating power of fabric. Windows enhanced with curtains become a focal point in a room, regardless of their architectural correctness. Being the most eye-catching element, they usually determine its decorative style. Thus it is essential in planning your window arrangement that it complements the proportions of the room.

Curtains are the feature in a room that offer the most opportunity for creativity. Their range of possibilities are wide because of the large historical repertoire from which one can take inspiration—from exceedingly lavish and twisted eighteenth-century silk concoctions to spare and tailored Art Nouveau creations. Historic painting and prints provide endless ideas for treating windows. To a great extent, elements borrowed from history are filtered through the medium of personal taste. The same look, say, French Empire, can be interpreted completely differently by any two individuals. You only have to know where to start.

OPPOSITE AND RIGHT: Curtains can add a lot of drama and interest to a room. These simple lavender taffeta curtains are enhanced with appliqué, which is made of several shades of purple faux suede cut in the shape of delphinium leaves. The leaves reinforce the theme of this room—a *jardin d'hiver*.

Chic Advice

The chief ingredients in any successful window treatment are imagination and knowledge. What to do, where, and how? To some extent there is a core repertoire of basic forms—a vocabulary of ideas from which professional designers tend to draw inspiration. First determine in which room you want to hang curtains. Obviously what you choose for a kitchen is going to be different from what you put in a living room or a bedroom. The key considerations are proportion, measurement, and detail.

Proportion

Proportion is vitally important. A classic window is half as wide as it is high. As much as possible use the window as a template for proportions. Sometimes, however, you will want the fabric to be proportioned differently in order to disguise an awkward shape. If the window seems too wide for its height, place the rod or pole higher than it would be normally. If in a same room you have various shapes of windows try to the extent possible to make uniform curtains or headings—pelmet, valance, or rod—as this will help unify the room. For example, if one of the windows is not floor length and has a radiator underneath, and the others are, such a window should nevertheless be treated as if it went to the floor with full-length curtains.

Some windows are beautiful in themselves, and the art in these cases is to ensure that the draping of the fabric enhances rather than hides the architectural framework. This is often true of picture windows. At its best, a picture window is a striking feature and needs little embellishment. Unfortunately, it lacks privacy and warmth and this often becomes an issue despite a breathtaking view. A large window can also be difficult to curtain successfully without the results looking like a stage set. Avoid large patterned fabrics. Choose a fabric and color that complement the walls. The best choice is a relatively subdued fabric, possibly a plain textured one.

When selecting the pattern and color of the curtain, you need to take into account not only the wall treatment but also the view through the window. The larger the area of fabric, the more important it is that it ties in well with other furnishing fabrics in the room. If full-length curtains need to be used, it is better to have them lined and interlined in order to give them more body, make them hang well, and improve their insulation qualities. If the view is unattractive, it is a good idea to screen it with a sheer fabric. It will then

OPPOSITE, CLOCKWISE FROM TOP LEFT: A tailored shade not only provides structure to a window but it is a clever way to dress it up. This window has a radiator below it and a wall of bookcases opposite making it virtually impossible for another type of decorative treatment. The scalloped edge adds a touch of whimsy as does the bright yellow silk, even more so when the sun shines trough creating a golden light. The painted and stenciled antique pelmet, which is identical to those on the rest of the room's windows, adds a polished appearance and a unifying look.

Curtains are an important decorative element as demonstrated in this billiard room. The soft classical cotton damask creates a feeling of warmth that is appropriate for this traditional gaming room. The heavy fringe contributes to a sense of coziness.

This yellow curtain is in the same room as the shade above. Made of the identical silk material and topped with a similar painted and stenciled pelmet, it is a window treatment that is successfully integrated with the others. The unusual curtain shape inspired by an eighteenth-century French window treatment works well in a tight space. It dresses up the French doors while not impeding on their movement.

The flowery linen fabric of the curtains seen here echoes the theme of this summer dining room overlooking the gardens. The room's walls are decorated with a collection of botanical watercolors. It is gracious to have the fabric puddle about one inch on the floor. Less fabric would look skimpy; more can become a safety hazard.

pleasantly diffuse the light, create a summery mood, and reduce the undesirable view to a soothing blur. Windows that are modest in dimension are also a perennial challenge.

The question that always needs to be asked is, does a small window need a curtain or shade at all? Usually some kind of window dressing is desirable, especially if it is in a bedroom. Curtains offer an excellent opportunity to correct a proportional imbalance. For example, you could extend the rod on each side to create extra width. A simple style will generate the most pleasing results. A rule of thumb is to opt for fabrics that are light in both weight and color, and to use plenty of material.

Measurement

Accurate measuring is an essential ingredient of success in any window dressing. There is nothing worse than having skimpy-looking curtains. If you are doing the work yourself, make sure that you are properly equipped. You will need a steel ruler to measure the window dimensions. Measure both vertical sides for curtain drops. In old houses especially, settling often causes the windows to become slightly distorted. A good way around the problem is to have fabric bunching on the floor. It looks better anyway and you will avoid having to make each curtain according to different measurements. Sometimes, however, you will need to use a level, especially for shades, to check accuracy. With any curtain, you need to decide on the degree of fullness required. Generally, you should allow two to two and a half times the finished width. Remember to add fabric for overlaps and returns if you are fitting curtains to a track.

Detail

Details make a great deal of difference. A fringe versus a braid or a trim, and all of a sudden, the look of the curtain is changed. It is crucial to pay close attention to all the details. A mistake—for example, an out-of-proportion rosette, uneven lengths, or carelessly finished hems—will be unattractive. To the visitor viewing the window dressing for the first time, the impact should be exactly as you intended it—a perfect match between conception and execution.

It is frequently the tie-backs that determine the overall finished form of curtains. For example, if curtains are hung in a pair so that a generous scoop of fabric forms when they are attached to the sides of a window, it will be the tie-back that keeps them there, creating a look of fullness. The most effective tie-backs are often the simplest. A long narrow strip of self-lined fabric, widening out at each end, makes an excellent tie-back that can be fastened casually around the curtain. The other option is the classic rope with a tassel at the end. The best way to hold it in place is with a small brass curtain ring.

If in doubt, keep your curtain scheme simple. Pay attention to proportion and choose quality fabric. *Bonne chance!*

Tie-backs help show off the shape and fullness of curtains. They are a perfect finishing touch. Placed properly, tie-backs let natural light pass through.

The Fireplace, Mantels & Mirrors

You are king by your own fireside, as much as any monarch in his throne.
—Miguel de Cervantes (1547–1616), from *Don Quixote de la Mancha*

FIREPLACE & MANTEL

The fireplace has always been the principal feature of a room, a source of warmth and light, and therefore by implication of life itself. Imagine a fireplace three hundred years ago in a cold and drafty château. Even with central heating, the fireplace still remains a focal point today.

It is only logical that architects spent a great deal of effort to design fireplaces to be as striking as possible. By the mid-1650s, separate sets of designs specifically for fireplaces became available in Paris. Jean Barbet's book *Livre d'Architecture,* featuring many fireplace variations, was so popular that it was reissued several times in the 1600s. The book was dedicated to the Cardinal de Richelieu and claimed to show

OPPOSITE: In the eighteenth century, a *trumeau* referred to a mirror combined with a painting above it, often placed over a fireplace mantel or a door. The example here is French, late eighteenth century.

RIGHT: A drawing called a *sanguine* for the dauphin's *appartement* at Versailles, c. 1680, shows a small, elegant fireplace, fashionable during the seventeenth century. From the album *Décoration intérieure et jardins de Versailles.* RMN. Photo: Gérard Blot.

ABOVE: A drawing by Nadia Wolinska of a living room that I designed and called *Jardin d'hiver céleste*, for the French Designer Showhouse, 2001, sponsored by *House & Garden*. The fireplace is made of sleek stainless steel.

OPPOSITE: This fireplace is made of stone and creates a strong focal point in the pool house. A refined 1950s mirror with a glass frame above lightens it up—a mixture of chic and rough.

Ce qu'il ya de plus beau dans Paris. A lofty goal!

The sixteenth-century *cheminée* was a massive, heavily architectural structure, with a large drafty opening. The seventeenth century in France saw the evolution of the fireplace, which became gradually smaller and more elegant, with a lower opening, limiting the potential for draft. All the architectural elements surrounding the fireplace became less overpowering, as seen in the engravings from Jean Le Pautre's *Cheminées à la Moderne*, published in 1661. Their design is more compact and the ornament on the chimneybreast simpler. The fireplace surround would eventually become a wood panel en suite with the walls and moldings following the paneling style. The architect François Blondel remarked in 1683, *L'on faisait cy, devant beaucoup de depense pour la structure et les ornmens des cheminées que l'on chargeoit excessivement. Mais presentement on les rends plus légerès, et l'on les trouve plus belles dans leur simplicité.* (Formerly one spent a lot for the structure and decoration of chimneypieces, which were too heavily decorated, but today they are lighter and appreciated much more in their present, cleaner state.)

The simplification of the fireplace saw a plethora of accessories (*le comble de l'ironie*) to enhance it. The smaller opening needed props to hold the logs inside the fireplace so it gave birth to *chenets* (from *chienette*, meaning small dog; hence the English term "fire-dogs"), often elaborate objects made of *ormolu* and designed by such masters as Charles Le Brun.

Fireplaces in the summer should be "garnished with green bowes or flowers," maintained Antoine de Courtin, author of *Le Nouveau Traité de la Civilité*, written in 1671. These *feuillards*, as they were called in France, were elaborate screens of greenery that could provide effective hiding places, as several naughty stories of the time make clear. For example, they were a good hiding place for a lover! Another way of filling up a fireplace in the summer and to prevent drafts and soot from entering the room was the chimney board. This canvas was

usually painted with a vase of flowers or a still life. Instead of canvas, chimney boards could also be faced with tapestry, embroidery, gilt or tooled leather, or paper.

Simpler mantels needed ornaments so the *garniture de cheminée* came about in the seventeenth century. First, it consisted of two or three porcelain vases. Later it became more elaborate and grew to five large vases. In the late eighteenth century the combination of a clock flanked by two matching candlesticks became another popular version of the *garniture*. This elegant way to dress up a mantelpiece is still used today.

The ultimate novelty associated with the fireplace was brought about by means of mirror glass. The first known example was in 1684 at Versailles, and in no other than in the *chambre du roi* (the king's room). Such a fashion spread! In the 1690s Pierre Le Pautre published engravings entitled *Cheminées et Lambris à la Mode*, showing mirrors above the fireplace. He explained that it was the new, fashionable way to decorate as was done in the Sun King's palace.

In 1697 the Swedish architect Nicodemus Tessin (always a perfect source of information related to French decoration and behavior) was advising Countess Piper on how to do her house in Stockholm in the latest French style and recommended: *Pour les chiminées je les ferrois de glaces du haut en bas, c'est le goût qui régne et qui est d'autant mieux fondé qu'avec 2 ou 4 bougies un appartement par la reverberation se trouve plus éclairé et plus guay qu'un autre avec 12.* (I would make the chimneypieces with mirrors from top to bottom. That is the taste that prevails here and is the more justified since with two or four candles in a room it is lighter and more cheerful than with twelve due to the reflection.)

At the time, the effect of candles above the fire reflected in a mirror was a major novelty, and surely it was breathtakingly beautiful. Mirrors above the fireplace were here to stay; with or without candles the effect has been dazzling for generations ever since. In fact, to this day it is commonplace in decorating to hang mirrors above a fireplace.

In 1699, Robert de Cotte, one of the king's architects, made another leap forward for interior decoration: He hung a large mirror—eighty-four by forty-two inches—at Marly (the latest royal project) above a mantel. From then on the habit stuck. Throughout the eighteenth and nineteenth centuries many design books featured engravings showing how to achieve the new look, which was baptized *cheminées à la Royale* or *cheminées à la Française*. Many houses began to have hanging mirrors facing each other across a drawing room. Edith Wharton in her book *The Decoration of Houses* refers to exactly that fashion: *Above the mantel, there was always a mirror with another of the same shape and size directly opposite; and the glittering perspective thus produced gave to the scene an air of fantastic unreality.* It was not long before decorators added mirrors in bedrooms, hallways, or all over the house to open up space and add some much needed sparkle. It is clear that we are still following the vision of the Sun King that started in the Galerie des Glaces in 1682.

A distinguished wood-carved mantel with a French painting hung above the fireplace.

MIRRORS

We all remember the fairy tale, *Blanche Neige* (*Snow White*). For centuries, women have been obsessed with their beauty, brushing their hair, combing it, and adding color and makeup to their face. A mirror is an essential element since it is the best way to look at your own reflection. But mirrors as we know them now did not always exist. Imagine life without them!

A discovery made around 1480 in a small glassworks in Venice established one of the most effective monopolies in European history. Though the world had known colored glass since 4 B.C. Renaissance Venetian glassmakers discovered the real secret to producing the flat mirror. Their breakthrough process consisted of blowing the glass into a cylindrical form that was cut longitudinally and placed in a heated chamber where it was flattened with a wooden tool. It was then backed with an amalgam of mercury and tin.

The clever Venetians invented, along with this basic process, the looking glass, as it was called until about 1875. The literature is full of references to the looking glass. Before that brilliant discovery, mirrors were mostly made of highly polished metal. The Romans occasionally made them of glass backed by lead or other metals. Later, in the Gothic period, they were generally small, made either of metal or glass, often set in ivory frames and lavishly carved. The reflection must have been muddy, but it was better than standing over a pond!

Until the end of the seventeenth century, the Venetians retained a virtual monopoly on making mirrors. During the Renaissance these mirrors cost more than an Old Master painting and were one of the most sought-after luxury products in all of Europe. Furthermore, the formula for making them was of such immense value that the doges of the Serene Republic of Venice decreed that divulging any information about their production an offense punishable by nothing less than death. In addition, they also forbade glassmakers to

travel outside the Republic. It worked. The Venetians virtually controlled the market for nearly two hundred years.

In 1650, a very famous mirror in France, one that was considered unimaginably huge at the time— twenty-four inches square—was owned by Nicolas Fouquet, Louis XIV's first

LEFT: A detail of a French eighteenth-century gilded mirror in the Rococo style.

OPPOSITE: The corner of a nineteenth-century gilded French mirror, located in a hallway.

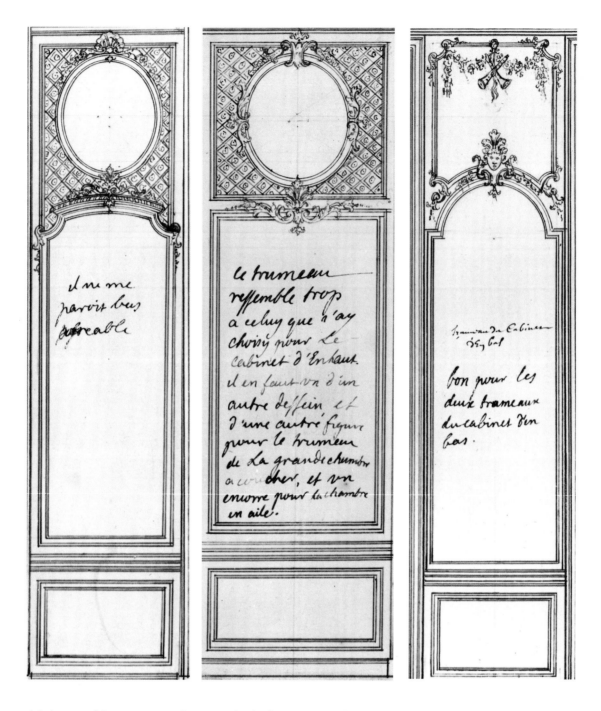

Ink drawing of three variations of *trumeaux*, by the *Dessinateur des Bâtiments du Roi*, Jules Hardouin-Mansart, probably for the Grand Trianon at Versailles in the mid-eighteenth century, all inscribed by Mansart. The term *trumeau* originally signified the space between two windows or doors. As shown in these drawings, *trumeaux* eventually were inset with mirrors. By the eighteenth century a looking glass with a painting above was used as an overmantel and was also called a *trumeaux*. National Museum, Stockholm.

finance minister. The early mirrors were available only to the wealthy because they were so expensive, but anyone who could afford one wanted one. Louis XIV, always ahead of the luxury curve, owned twenty-nine original makeup mirrors. Soon he realized the show-stopping potential of a public display of shimmering glass, but he was not about to continue to enrich the Venetian coffers at his expense. So Colbert, the king's new finance minister, set about luring skilled mirror makers to France. A secret war with Venice ensued.

By 1665, the *Manufacture Royale des Glaces de Miroirs* was established in the Faubourg Saint-Antoine, the Parisian center for furniture since the Middle Ages, and was given a complete monopoly over mirror making in France. The company still exists today and is known as Saint Gobain.

Chic Advice

Mirrors come in all shapes, from rectangular to oval or square, and were originally hung on walls above doorways and over mantels. Mirrors toward the second quarter of the seventeenth century could even be convex. This shape was first seen in France, and by the beginning of the eighteenth century this fashion had spread to the rest of Europe and America.

When selecting antique mirrors, remember that old glass is very thin, seldom exceeding $3/16$ of an inch. Keep in mind that modern glass is $1/4$ to $3/8$ of an inch thick, nearly double that of old glass. Also, old glass reflects a yellow or gray tone, while the reflection in modern glass is colorless. Keep in mind that early mirrors were silvered with mercury and tin. Modern glass is coated on the back with a brick red lacquer.

An expensive component of the mirror became its frame, which was often gilded and carved according to the fashion of the day, and went from the Baroque and Rococo to Neoclassical, Empire, and Federal styles. At the end of the seventeenth century, painted decoration largely supplanted carvings on mirrors. The frames often were decorated to match the wallpaper, especially in bedrooms or bedchambers. Later, during the eighteenth century, delicately carved decorations on mirrors were carefully thought out to blend with marble mantels and even the whole room. This ornamentation was generally carried out to match the plasterwork of the walls and, as a consequence, such mirrors are seldom found in perfect condition.

A good way to differentiate between frames and mirrors is their size. Picture frames made later on into mirrors usually are too square. They have about half the value of a mirror in its original frame. Also mirrors always have a wooden backing; paintings do not. Restorations to an old mirror will not detract from its value. Re-gilding of the frame is often a necessary evil and is not a problem if it is well done. Do not brush on shiny gold paint! It is rare to find a delicately carved mirror frame without breakage. Perfect condition is often the evidence of later work or, even worse, a fake. *Un faux—quelle horreur!*

Place the mirror above a mantel. It is the classic way, and always an elegant enhancement, as history has taught us. However, you can play with mirror sizes, selecting from very small to gigantic ones. Mirror size will change the mood and scale of the room. Hang a collection of mirrors of different sizes for a whimsical effect. If you do not have a mantel in the living room and need to create some focus, you can hang a very large mirror—even a completely oversized one. It's a good trick.

In a small dining room, consider adding a mirrored ceiling; it will reflect the light, especially when the room is lit with candles (the "Hall of Mirrors" effect). In a small foyer or entry, a good way to open up the space and hide doors is to cover them with antique glass panels. The effect, a classic, is always good. Mirror on mirror is also chic. For example, a mirrored wall in a hallway can be enhanced by hanging a mirror on top of the surface. This effect is *très chic* in a bathroom. *Bonne chance!*

On May 6, 1682, the *Mercure de France* announced that the seat of the French government was now at Versailles. On December 1, 1682, the Sun King gave a grand housewarming party at which he opened the Galerie des Glaces to the public—the last mirror having been installed the night before! Jean Donneau de Vise not surprisingly devoted the lead article in the December 1682 issue of his newspaper *Le Mercure Galant* to the new *galerie*. He marveled that "they multiplied a million times over the gallery's size, so it seems to have no end." The same year, Claude Saugrain's guide pronounced Versailles "the eighth wonder of the world" and the Hall of Mirrors as "the most enchanting sight known to man."

Louis XIV had succeeded at creating a dazzling environment for himself and his court and deserved his attribution as the Sun King. From now on, all of his important diplomatic meetings were to take place in the Galerie des Glaces (as numerous paintings can attest) in order to suitably impress his guests. Louis XIV had pulled off a display of glass on a scale never seen before—seventeen expanses of mirrored glass (each almost eighteen feet high and over six and a half feet wide). Directly across from each mirror stood an equally large window through which the equally beautiful garden can be seen, a feast for the eyes indeed—*une fête pour les yeux!* It is also important to note that in 1682 for the first time visitors were able to get a reflection of themselves from head to toe.

By 1687, the glass-making process had changed. Glass was no longer blown but poured onto tables of all sizes to create a flat mirrored surface. This new process was the springboard that catapulted Saint Gobain to world dominance. It made possible the production of looking glasses of much greater size and regularity of surface. Mirrors subsequently became widely available, and so the cost fell. Without this revolutionary technique, the mirror would never have become a central element in interior decoration accessible for all of us. In 1696, *L'art de la verrerie*, the first comprehensive study of both glass making and mirror making, was published. In it mirrors are described as "the most glorious of all works of art."

From the start of the eighteenth century French mirrors were exported all over Europe. Louis XIV's gamble had worked. Design clearly owes a large debt to this showman of a monarch. Where would *le style français* be without him?

OPPOSITE: Detail of a French eighteenth-century gilded mirror in the Rococo style.

RIGHT: Detail of an American gilded mirror in the Neoclassical style.

Light & Lighting Fixtures

C'est la nuit que notre foi en la lumière est admirable.

(It is at night that faith in light is admirable.)

—Edmond Rostand (1868–1918), *Chantecler,* 1907

IT IS DIFFICULT TO IMAGINE today just how little light our ancestors had at night, and just how inconvenient candles were. The best way to experience this today is when a power outage descends on the area where you live. It is not exactly fun! *Pas drôle du tout!* Candles are not exactly easy to use either. Their flickering light moves, creating areas of darkness and shadows, and highlighting pieces of furniture and objects in a relatively erratic manner.

Good wax candles were expensive and other forms of lighting—tallow candles and rush lights—were either smelly, quickly consumed, or both. Tallow candles (*chandelles*) were made half of beef fat and half of refined mutton fat. In Paris, at any rate, one was not permitted to add pork fat, since that was particularly pungent. *Chandelles* had to be constantly watched when in use. They gave an uneven light and had to be snuffed so that they did not smoke and smell, which invariably happened when they were extinguished. *Quelle horreur!* Rush lights were made of peeled meadow rushes soaked in fat. So they had an unpleasant smell too. As an indication, a rush light fourteen inches long would burn in about half an hour. You needed a lot of them for a night!

OPPOSITE: Lanterns come in many forms and shapes.

RIGHT: A pair of French eighteenth-century *ormolu* candlesticks.

Beeswax candles (*bougies*) were brighter and burned evenly. They were not malodorous, and their wick required little snuffing, as they did not dribble down the side. So *bougies* were much better, but much more expensive. Jean du Pradel, in his *Traité contre le luxe* of 1705, contrasts the simple tastes of yesteryear when people had been content to burn *chandelles,* at four *sous* per pound, while during the extravagant eighteenth century one burned wax candles—*bougies*—costing twenty-two *sous* per pound. A big difference!

When a large number of *bougies* were lit for a special occasion, it was duly noted and remarked on with delight, as Nicodemus Tessin did in his letters back to Sweden. He wrote that at a ball given in the Galerie des Glaces, at Versailles in 1695, there were seven thousand *bougies*. Quite a number! It was an unusual event even at the king's court. However, the effect must have been breathtaking with the lights reflected again and again by dozens of mirrors.

Because candles had to be lit and snuffed out, they were normally set at a convenient height, between table and shoulder level. The light, in fact, often was at eye level and therefore reflected the front of furniture and objects rather than their top surface, in contrast to today. It created a sense of intimacy regardless of the size of the room.

ABOVE: A pair of late-eighteenth century French carved wood candlesticks adorned with roosters, which are quite rare for the obvious reason.

OPPOSITE: A *garniture de cheminée*, consisting of a pair of American-designed candelabra, representing the tree of life.

All those *chandelles* and *bougies* had to be held and displayed. So candleholders were created. There are really only three principal types of candleholders: the candlestick, which may be placed on a flat surface; the sconce, which hangs on the wall; and the chandelier, which is suspended from the ceiling. The word *chandelier* comes from the French (of course!) and means holder for *chandelles*. But later on, chandeliers usually held *bougies,* because of their higher quality. Candlesticks with arms (*bras*) are called candelabra, literally meaning tree of candles.

In a house of any standing, many forms of candlesticks existed. Wooden ones were usually found in the kitchen and the working quarters. In *salons* and reception rooms silver candlesticks or *bougeoirs* (meaning having a *bougie*) became fashionable as well as with *ormolu*. By the way, the English term "ormulu" is based directly on the French word *ormolu* (powdered gold), which was warmed before being applied to the bronze. The technique was of French origin and at the beginning of the nineteenth century was still mainly a Parisian specialty. There were many variants of the standard form, including the chamber candlestick, which stood in a large drip pan with a handle, or the *bougeoirs à la financière*, which were presumably specially suited for office work. Cardinal Mazarin owned few of these. The height of this type of candle was adjustable, and it had a shade.

The standard form of early sconces had one or more branches springing from the lowest point of a reflecting back-plate. It often took the form of a copper dish that was suspended on the wall by a ring at the back. During the mid-seventeenth century, this design went out of fashion and other sconce shapes became popular. Sometimes they were fitted with reflectors made of mirror glass, and increasingly sconces (*appliqués*) were made of wood, painted or gilded, and later included silver or *ormolu*.

Chandeliers, whether lit or not, constituted an important decorative feature in a room, so considerable attention was paid to their embellishment. In inventories chandeliers are invariably the most expensive items. In order to obtain as much sparkle as possible, reflecting surfaces were gradually introduced. The most striking seventeenth-century innovation sprung from the use of rock crystal, which reflected the light beautifully. Beads of this material, globular or faceted, were threaded onto wire armatures to form arms or were linked together to form chains. The French (once again!) developed the rock-crystal chandelier to its fullest splendor.

Chandeliers made of rock crystal came to be called *lustres,* and this subsequently became the generic term for all chandeliers. It is interesting to note that candles were normally only fitted into the nozzles of a chandelier when they were about to be lit. Occasionally in paintings one sees a single candle left, probably to serve in an emergency. Chandeliers with their branches surrounded by mirrors are called lanterns. They were also highly prized in the eighteenth century. Originally used to illuminate hallways and staircases, lanterns were

OPPOSITE, CLOCKWISE FROM TOP LEFT: A crystal chandelier in the recognizably French style—just a more recent version.

A sconce in the shape of a lantern—this one is a Colonial Williamsburg reproduction.

A pair of wooden sconces, enhanced with gold paint made to imitate an *ormolu* effect—the pauper version of gilding.

A wall sconce made of glass and gilded metal. Although modest, it is very charming.

BELOW: A late-seventeenth-century ink drawing of a French hall lantern, possibly made of sheet metal and glass. National Museum, Stockholm.

RIGHT: A nineteenth-century metal and glass lantern in the Gothic style.

OPPOSITE: This Chinese-inspired hanging lantern fills in the large space and adds a touch of whimsy.

soon placed in dining rooms. One reason for this development may have been that before the invention of dining rooms, people were in the habit of eating in antechambers. Soon the price of a beautiful lantern was as high as the price of a *lustre*. From the middle of the eighteenth century, the lantern clearly (no pun intended) had the royal seal of approval.

During Louis XVI's reign, cylindrical lanterns were in use, evidence that the technique of making curved mirrors was known at the time. Nevertheless, despite the variety of candleholders, in fact, the strongest light in a room after dark would mostly come from the fire. With the fireplace playing such an important part, the surrounding of the mantel became the focal point of the decor of a room in the evening because it was the only thing that one could see. It created a real sense of intimacy. The marble mantel gleamed, the *chenets* came alive, and the mirror sparkled, reflecting the faint rays of the golden light.

The advent of electricity drastically changed the way of life and the way rooms in houses looked at night. Today, lighting is just as significant a part of your planned decoration as your color scheme, rugs, curtains, or wallpaper. It is only through correct lighting that your color scheme comes alive at night instead of sinking into drab grayness. *Un desastre à éviter*—a disaster to avoid.

It is also only through light adequately distributed that one can read or work at night without eyestrain. It is important to create a balance—to know when to use the romantic candlelight of our ancestors and when to take full advantage of the modern technology. Lamps and lighting fixtures are now as much decorative accessories as candles were in the past. They need to match your need and your decor. *Bonne chance!*

An example of the famous *bouillote* lamp—a typical French creation—just spiced up a bit with aged orange paint. A cheap-chic trick.

Chic Advice

- Cove lighting is an efficient and dramatic way to give light to a room. It is excellent in a dining room, for example, using a dimmer. It provides a soft ambient light.

- Spotlights should always be used with a dimmer. They are great in rooms with high ceilings or in a kitchen or bathroom, where a strong light is needed at times.

- Another dramatic effect can be achieved by putting luminous panels on top of a bookcase, hidden by molding. They diffuse a soft glow throughout a room.

- Candlelight is wonderful in a dining room, providing that you have some extra lighting to help enhance it (if possible, using a dimmer).

- Floor lamps are tricky. Unless they are perfect for your decoration scheme, avoid them.

- Table lamps provide a natural and livable light in a room. Try to use them for a living room or library, or in bedrooms placed on bedside tables. However, be sure to use large enough table lamps. Make sure that the table that supports them is of the right size and not too small.

- Shades should be proportioned to the base of a lamp. A sophisticated shade will immediately enhance a simple lamp. Remember high and low. However, a cheap shade on a sophisticated lamp will kill the effect.

- Lamps in a grouping, for example on either side of a sofa, should be of the same height.

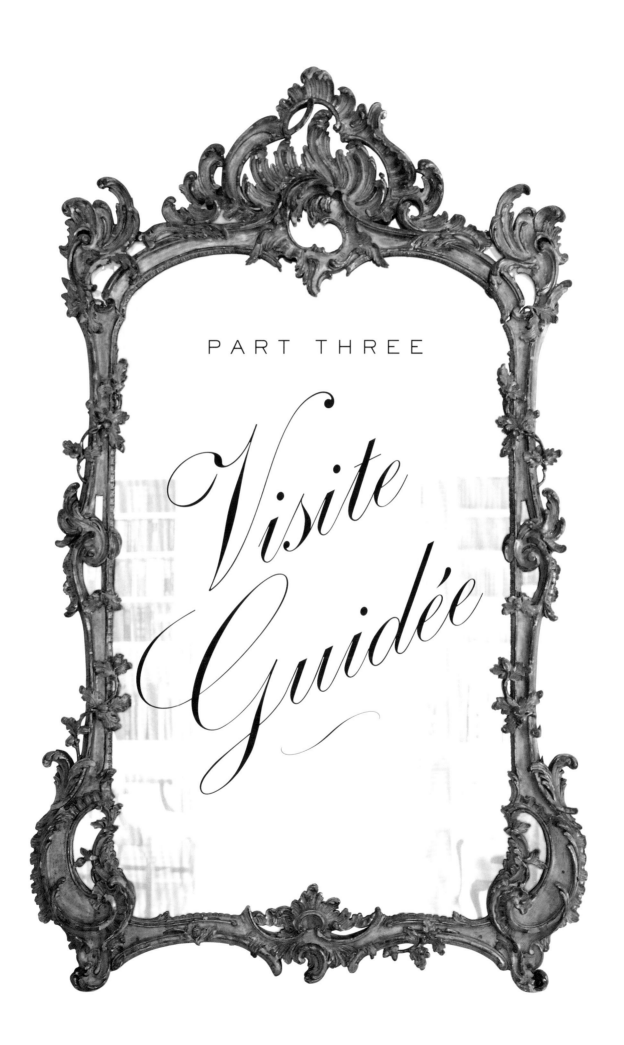

PART THREE

Visite Guidée

The Entrance, Hall & Stairs

Les architectes sont tous des idiots, ils oublient toujours de mettre des escaliers.

(Architects are all idiots; they always forget to put in the stairs.)

—Gustave Flaubert (1821–80)

ENTRANCES, HALLS, AND STAIRS are the oldest elements in architectural history. They appear to change with each era, reflecting the prevailing philosophy, way of life, and symbols of their time. Entrances and halls are essential: They give the first impression of a building, and we all know how crucial a first impression is— *très importante. Escaliers* (stairs) are the framework of a building, its skeleton. Stairs represent and respond to the society for which they are built.

Early medieval halls were versatile and cavernous spaces, which had to serve many functions depending on the time or the occasion. Using fabric, a *fourrier* (the man in charge of fabrics for a *seigneur*, a nobleman) could partition off part of the great hall to make a smaller, more intimate area, rig up a dais and canopy where the lord could sit in state, or prepare for the staging of the buffet with cupboard cloth. *Tapisseries* (tapestries) could be hung to hide doors. They generally dressed and warmed up the vast space, and protected guests from drafts during ceremonial banquets. Sometimes the great hall was even transformed into sleeping quarters. It was a versatile room indeed!

Gradually, as society became more stable and life became a little bit easier for a larger segment of the population, hall designs changed. Halls became smaller. By the end of the sixteenth century, there was a hall at the entrance. It was often where the servants ate, supervised by the steward, who was the chief officer of the household. In the late seventeenth century, halls became synonymous with the entrance; the multipurpose aspect tended to disappear. Their main function was as a sort of waiting room. A handbook of 1675 explained which decorations were most suitable for halls, and even described their placement. Apparently, for some

PAGE 120: Ma Maison, a view from the back.

OPPOSITE: Welcome! The entrance is spacious, with its high ceiling and enhanced by aqua-colored walls.

123

RIGHT: The architectural details are simple and beautiful. The carpet makes the entrance and stairs more whimsical and is, by the way, very resistant to the continual traffic of dogs and humans of all sizes.

OPPOSITE: The mahogany staircase baluster, cumulating in a sophisticated spiral handrail, is supported by a carved newel post, which gives strength and elegance to the entrance.

strange reason paintings adorned with shepherds, flocks of sheep, peasants, and milkmaids were considered ideal. *Pourquoi pas!*

Halls needed to impress, look luxurious, and withstand heavy traffic. So the habit of using stone or marble for the floors of châteaux developed. Black-and-white marble was a staple, as was cream-colored limestone, similar to that used in many of the facades of classical châteaux. For even grander schemes, a hall might have marble- or limestone-covered walls, which were also sometimes enhanced with columns, niches, or arches.

Grand stairs and staircases, or *escaliers d'honneur,* were often made of light-colored stone or marble, for the same practical and aesthetic reasons. Throughout history, many staircases stand out because of either their

engineering ingenuity, sheer beauty, or both. Most French architectural landmarks boast special or even extraordinary staircases. Their style and construction varies with the centuries, along with their use and location. The famous Notre Dame Cathedral in Paris, which was built during the twelfth century, has not only one, but two beautiful helical (spiral) stairs located in each of its towers. It was quite an accomplishment at the time. The stairs are still standing proud and tall, their treads springing from the newel in a sinuous curve like the petals of a flower unfolding. *C'est très beau.* Other remarkable staircases are studded throughout the well-known Châteaux de la Loire. Azay-le-Rideau and Chenonceau, both legendary sixteenth-century castles, have innovative and outstanding main staircases with straight flights of steps amid barrel-vaulted ceilings with classical coffering. At Chenonceau, the main staircase leads to spiral stairs, enhanced with a balustrade that sheds light into the whole staircase. *Remarquable!* These two superb staircases gave a foretaste of the functional and aesthetic importance of *escaliers* in France in later periods—from the Château de Blois to Versailles. Blois was the first example of a spiral staircase with outside balconies, which enabled the court to watch performances in the courtyard below. This type of staircase (usually a bit simpler), with a single helix, was to become commonplace and always had a decorative purpose.

By far, the most famous of the double-helix stairs is at the Château de Chambord, near Blois. It is attributed to none other than Leonardo da Vinci. The extraordinary feature of this staircase is that it is treated like a building in its own right, and has a diameter of almost thirty feet. The hollow stairwell with its twenty-four tiny windows, enabled people walking up and down the staircase to see where they were going, but more important, it allowed light to flood the stairs from outside. Leonardo's notes and sketches show his fascination with stairs and shell shapes. His interest, as in many of his inventions, is practical as well as creative. For example, for public stairs leading to the streets, he recommends the use of a spiral staircase and comments: *It should be round because in the corners of square ones nuisances are apt to be committed.* So true!

The relocation of the principal rooms of the palaces (or châteaux) from their traditional location on the ground floor to the first floor made the entrance stairway of the Baroque era of greater functional importance. So it is not surprising that the staircase grew in size and magnificence. Louis XIV used architecture and its theatrical effect as a political tool. A great example was l'Escalier des Ambassadeurs for the palace at Versailles. The grand staircase was intended, as its name indicated, for the use of ambassadors ascending to the Galerie des Glaces for an audience with Louis XIV. Visiting dignitaries could be received on the stairs and where they were greeted was a measure of their rank and social position. The bottom flight, called *palier de repos*, flowed out from the landing in all directions. The entire staircase was decorated with marble inlays, gilded bronze, painting, sculpture, *trompe l'oeil* windows, and niches. Quite a sight, apparently. Unfortunately it was destroyed in 1752.

Long after reception rooms had ceased to be located on the second floor, the grand staircase, the stairs, and the entrance hall remained

A wide-angle view of the staircase shows off its nice proportions.

popular, part of the trappings of status, an element *extérieur de richesse*. We learn through César Daly (1811–94) in his *Architecture privée au XIX siècle*, published in 1872 in Paris, that in upper-class apartment buildings the staircase was intended to create an immediate impression, as had also been the case in the *hôtels particuliers* or châteaux of the seventeenth and eighteenth centuries. It was not simply a functional space, but a focus of display. This accounts for the elaborate banister, lamps, and statues that usually decorated stairs at this time. Bourgeois buildings of the nineteenth century rose no higher than five stories, with three of impressive proportion. *Appartements* on the second through fourth floors were connected by an imposing stone staircase. Wooden stairs, marking a diminished social status, led from the top of the staircase to the fifth floor, which was inhabited by less well-to-do families. The sixth floor, often a converted attic, if it existed at all, was for the *chambres de bonnes* (maids' rooms) and was also linked by a wooden staircase. There was also a service staircase, located either alongside the main staircase or at the rear of the building. The service staircase, always of wooden construction (*bien sur!*), provided access to the kitchens on every floor as well as to the maids' quarters below the roof.

Today's celebrated staircases, made of modern materials such as steel, often take inspiration from the past. For example, the helical stair at the Louvre in Paris, designed by I. M. Pei, is even located inside a pyramid! This shows that the past is alive and well, a constant source of inspiration and amazement.

Chic Advice

Make the most of the hall, especially if you are crowded for space. If a hall is spacious enough to be furnished and still have room for traffic, there is no reason why a console or side table cannot be placed in it. These pieces are both useful and attractive. If you have the space, try a seat, which is always practical, as well.

◆ An interesting point is that the suggested distance between steps does not seem to be dictated anywhere. It is one of the few things in building design to have escaped codification. *Miracle ou désastre?* Always try to make the distance between steps the same; otherwise, it is really dangerous. It is a real hazard if their distance varies because you lose your footing.

◆ Be careful to not make your stairs an obstacle course. Avoid loose carpets, wobbly steps, shaky balusters, or too steep steps.

◆ Spiral (helical) stairs have the great advantage of taking up very little space.

The abundance of tall plants contributes to the spacious feeling and gives a relaxed atmosphere to an otherwise somewhat grand space. The family dog, Bling-bling, happily mugs for the camera.

The Salon

Le marquis ouvrit la porte du salon; une des dames se leva (la marquise elle-même),

vint à la rencontre d'Emma et la fit asseoir pres d'elle, sur une causeuse,

où elle se mit a lui parler amicalement, comme si elle l'a connaissait depuis longtemps.

(The marquis opened the door of the living room;

one of the women stood up [the marquise herself],

she came to meet Emma, asked her to sit next to her on a small sofa

where she started to talk to her amicably as old friends.)

—Gustave Flaubert (1821–80), *Madame Bovary,* 1857

HERE IS HOW THE *SALON*—the reception room, or what we today call the living room—came about. In the grand châteaux around 1600, the reception room leading to the state bedchamber was called the great chamber. The name for this room soon changed to *salon*. At Versailles, *les grands appartements du roi* boasted an impressive suite of *salons*: the Salon de l'Abondance, de Venus, de Diane, de Mars, de Mercure, and finally, d'Apollon (the brightest of all the planets and the emblem of the king). In this palace one *salon* was not enough for containing and impressing the large numbers of beribboned courtiers. In 1710, a seventh *salon* was added— the Salon d'Hercule. Throughout the seventeenth and early eighteenth centuries the tendency was to increase the number of reception rooms. *Quelle surprise!* Each of them was assigned a special usage; there was the audience chamber, the throne room, and the Salon des Ambassadeurs, among others.

Those large, imposing, ultrasophisticated reception rooms were enhanced with painted ceilings, marble chimneys, *parquet à la française,* silver *torchères* and candelabra, side tables, porcelain, paintings, mirrors, orange trees, and very few seats—as no one could sit in the presence of the king. The few armchairs were *fauteuils à la reine*—meaning *fauteuils* that were intended to be placed against wood paneling, with straight, often oval-shaped backs and low seats. In a word, those beautiful *salons* were not cozy places where you could loll around and put your feet up. It was standing room only! They soon led to the creation of *cabinets*, or private *salons*, which were the forerunners of the *petits appartements* so dear to the eighteenth century, where life could go on in a more informal manner.

This view of the *salon* (living room) shows an interesting mix of furnishings. The French daybed in the Neoclassical style is made of painted metal, the French mirror is Louis XV period, very Rococo, and the lamps are Chinese. On one of the side tables sits a French *rafraichissoire* and on the other an American painted piece. It all works beautifully. *Miracle!*

Versailles's inventories are full of drawings, most of them designs for the dauphin's *appartement* and *salons* of 1690, showing wing chairs, *canapés pour se reposer* (sofas for taking a nap), and *fauteuils* with curtains, all tufted and cozy-looking. Such furnishings made the dauphin's rooms one of the marvels of the palace at the time. Comfort in the *salon* as we know it today was invented then. Thus the word "salon" became also synonymous with a gathering of *beaux esprits*—the cultured people. The *salons* trained men to be sensitive to feminine aspirations and women to be responsive to masculine intelligence. In these gatherings conversation became an art pushed to a level of excellence never before seen. Many men and women often ascribed the largest part of their education to this kind of social discourse. Ninon de Lenclos opened her celebrated salon in 1657. It became one of the most celebrated *salons*. Men of letters, music, art, politics, and wars, along with their wives, exchanged ideas and *bons mots*. It was the crowning charm of French society. In this regard, the period from 1660 to 1760 in France marked a zenith of civilization.

Under Louis XV, life became more informal, and as Voltaire tells us: *Today, social behavior is easier than in the past . . . ladies can be seen reading on sofas or day beds without causing embarrassment to their friends and acquaintance.* The eighteenth century was an era dominated by pleasure, luxury, and frivolity. Small comfortable *salons* where *gens de qualité*

TOP: The shape of the *salon* is quite awkward so the challenge was to create several welcoming seating areas. To warm up the space, the walls were painted a deep yellow with white trim accents.

LEFT: Mix texture and pattern—for example, rough felt appliqué with fine printed linen and cotton *moiré*—to make your room come alive.

OPPOSITE: The French doors of the *salon* open onto the purple garden room. The parquet floor is kept carpet-free to show off its beauty.

LEFT: Details in the *salon*—the intricate wooden floor and the French Neoclassical daybed ready for a cozy nap.

ABOVE: A view of the room's focal point—the mantelpiece of the fireplace embellished with a pair of American girandole, and a collection of turtles, some of precious stone and others made by friends or my children. A French painting in a gilt frame that hangs above it is this decorative ensemble's finishing touch.

RIGHT: Another medley of interesting, cheap, and chic objects—from a lollipop Ami Pierrot tin box to eighteenth-century potpourri and a funny music box.

FRAMES: GILDED OR NOT?

We all know that a painting, even a drawing, looks hundreds of times better with a frame, any frame. All of a sudden a relatively simple decoration becomes substantial, worthy of being hung on the wall of our *salon*. A frame makes a major difference to a loose piece of paper or a canvas. A painting, even by Picasso, without a frame, would be rather sloppily applied to a wall! Imagine Leonardo da Vinci's *Mona Lisa* proudly displayed in the Louvre in Paris without a frame—*impossible!*

A picture frame immediately gives importance, structure, and definition to the art it frames; hence its name. It is also the finishing touch in a *salon*. In most cases (unless it is contemporary, nonfigurative art like my friend Nabil Nahas's highly textured paintings, which have no frames) a painting is not really finished until it is framed. Frames function as decorative borders, as

support, and also as protection for paintings or watercolors, which are very fragile. Although the frame is the enhancer, the reflector of light, and the border, it adds both value and visual importance to the painting, which should never compete with it. The frame intentionally separates the work from the external environment—wall color, room size, light source—and creates a discrete visual effect. Done properly it enriches the work of art and enhances its value.

In an interesting twist a good frame gives a second-rate painting a rich, more valuable appearance; it does the same for a good painting, and makes the package even more appealing. Therefore, frames are used to increase the marketability of pictures. It is quite amazing to notice how much better pictures sell when in handsome, rich, frames. Presentation in everything counts and a good first impression helps as much in art as in life. Artists have always realized that the frames for their paintings were important marketing tools as well as an aesthetic statement. Many of them designed or chose the frames for their paintings, often paying hefty fees—money they did not necessarily have—to satisfy their clients.

Hardly any frame before the fifteenth century still exists today. Until that time most paintings were executed upon wooden panels, which were set in a molded framework with the solid-panel and frame being all of one piece. Early pictures were usually furnished

LEFT: The lovely botanicals around the summer dining room are yet another chic and cheap trick. They look like antique collectibles but in fact they have been photocopied from various books onto sepia paper and have been placed in identical inexpensive frames.

OPPOSITE: This frame is recognizable as a picture frame, as opposed to a mirror frame, because of its shape.

with curtains or even sometimes with wooden shutters: if you had seen enough of a painting you drew the curtains, or closed the shutters. *Pourquoi pas?*

Most remaining early frames were often gilded and sometimes enriched with precious stones. Like earlier models, frames in the mid- to late nineteenth century were exclusively composed of a basic wood foundation to which inner linings and outer moldings were added. Frequently they were overlaid with ornamentation made of composition (a moldable substance consisting of whiting, resin, and oil, glued to the frame). Once the ornamentation was attached to the wood base, the whole frame was smoothed over with gesso (a composition of gypsum, linseed oil, and glue). An undercoat of red, blue, yellow, or gray gilder clay was then added to enrich the tone of the traditional gold-leaf finish that was then applied.

Two basic gilding techniques, one using water and the other oil, provided contrasting effects of high gloss and matte finish. In

Paintings can be hung together in groupings or separately but this depends on the size of your walls. If you choose to create groupings, make sure the paintings complement one another and the frames work well together.

water gilding a mixture of alcohol, water, and hide glue is applied to a layer of bole (a fine-grained clay substance used as a base for gilding). This adhesive would then hold the gold leaf laid onto it. Once dry, the frame could be burnished. *Voilà*.

Oil gilding consists of an oil-based mixture applied to the bole, to which the gilding is applied. Oil gilding cannot be burnished and thus retains a matte surface. Gilded frames, with various embellishments and finishes as fashions changed, seem to be a common thread throughout countries and centuries.

Around the middle of the seventeenth century, pictures, especially portraits, were frequently enclosed within moldings, either plain or enriched, forming elements of the then almost universally paneled wall surfaces. By the end of the seventeenth century, philosopher Robert Boyle (1627–91) mentioned the use of papier mâché for picture frames in a publication. During the eighteenth and early nineteenth centuries this material was used extensively for this purpose throughout Europe.

Ensuing decades saw the fashion for oval frames soar; other periods reverted to the classical rectangular shape, with or without heavy carvings. This large variety of picture frames in history allows us today to be able to choose from a generous inventory of designs. Many mediums are used for frames nowadays, permitting a range of pricing. It is very liberating—you can choose what you like and what matches your pocketbook. *Quelle chance!* Remember, paintings are the finishing touch of a *salon*, like lipstick on a woman.

Chic Advice

- You can improve an old frame or a simple, inexpensive one with a couple of easy tricks. Paint is often the best disguise. Choose a luxurious dark brown or a deep red and edge it in gold. You will have instantly a very chic frame.

- Another favorite of mine is to use cutouts. Out of old magazines, cut three or four images that you will apply to your frame. Glue them on, and then cover with a transparent varnish. If you feel adventurous, you can always finish it off with a matching color for the edge. This is simple and fun for photographs.

- Frames can look beautiful and so can what they hold. However, it is a common mistake to hang frames too high.

Frame Terminology

- Back edge: The outermost section of the frame.

- Ogee: A molding featuring a combination of convex and concave lines in an S-shape.

- Butt joint: A joint formed by two lengths of wood joined together and secured by plates.

- Butterfly key: A shaped piece of wood inset onto the back of a frame to secure a miter.

- Lap joint: A corner joint in which the end pieces of wood are partially cut away to overlap smoothly.

- Miter joint: The simplest and most common of joints—made by fastening together parts with the ends cut at an angle.

- Mortise and tenon: Joinery in which one piece of wood has a notch or hole cut into it to receive a projecting piece of wood.

would meet, play cards, read aloud, gamble, and flirt were all the rage, in addition to the intellectual salons mentioned before. For that purpose many *canapés*, (or sofas) bearing exotic and amusing names such as *canapé à medaillon*, *en gondole*, *en corbeilles*, *à joues*, appeared. The endless search for comfort stimulated the creation of new models.

These rooms were masterpieces of decor. Madame de Pompadour's rooms at Bellevue, her little gem of a château outside Paris, were regarded as remarkable. Madame de Pompadour, Louis XV's favorite and a major patron of the arts, had her *salon* decorated with spectacular carved *boiserie* by Veerbeckt, the best wood sculptor of the time. In addition, she commissioned Boucher, her favorite painter, to fit some paintings over the wood-paneled doors as well as to produce easel paintings, such as the *Toilette de Venus* (today in the Metropolitan Museum of Art, New York). Aubusson and the Gobelins

ABOVE: A side view of the *salon* in the pool house, with its varied green-and-white color scheme, sophisticated objects, such as the marble and terra-cotta eighteenth-century bust, and simple, practical, white duck Crate & Barrel sofas.

OPPOSITE: A detail view of the *salon* illustrating my design philosophy to a T: simple sofas enhanced with custom-made pillows, framed photocopied coral prints next to rare Nabil Nahas paintings, and flea market finds intermingled with unusual Wedgwood and terra-cotta.

provided tapestries and carpets. To finish off the furniture, there were exquisite *vernis martin* pieces. Carved and gilded mirrors reflected dozens of candles and the delicate Sèvres porcelain that Madame de Pompadour was so fond of and added yet another layer of sophistication. Curtains from Lyon were of the palest silk, with fringes and braids; with them the decoration was complete. From then on, all the decorative elements needed to create a *salon* were established: curtains, mantel, mirror, carpet, paintings, precious objects, candelabra, porcelain, furniture, *canapés*, *fauteuils*, and chairs.

A classical house in the eighteenth century had at least two *salons*: *un grand* and *un petit*. The *grand salon* was for entertaining visiting guests, while the *petit* usually was more for family members or reading. For major social events such as a ball, a château usually had a ballroom and a *galerie* for paintings and portraits, in addition to a billiard room, a dining room, and, of course, a library and a *chapelle*.

In the nineteenth century, a well-appointed *appartement* was simply inconceivable without a *salon*—a theatrical space *par excellence,* it was the scene of the social ritual that linked the old aristocracy to the new growing

ABOVE: A green-and-white cotton pillow has been added to the velvet upholstered chair in the pool house *salon*. Cotton and velvet—once again, high and low.

RIGHT: A front view of the pool house *salon* with my favorite mix of high and low—antiques and flea market finds. In the foreground is a late-nineteenth-century Louis XVI-style chair that has been painted white and is upholstered in a chic, fun manner—with purple-pink embroidered flowers.

bourgeoisie. The *salon* was where the lady of the house received her guest on a fixed day (*le jour de visite*). Thus the custom of visiting had begun, which was modeled after the famous intellectual salons of the seventeenth and eighteenth centuries of Madame de Scudery or Mesdames de La Sablière and de Lambert, the latter a follower of Ninon de Lenclos.

The *grand salon* of the Napoleon III period (and even after) often had at the center a round *borne* or a *pouf*. The writer Théophile Gautier describes this innovative decor: *What could be more charming than a group of women of different and contrasting beauty seated on a pouf in the center of a salon in a billow of guipures and lace which froths at their feet like the sea at the feet of Venus.* These words could describe the painting by Franz Xavier Winterhalter, *Eugénie avec les dames de sa court*. It was a *grand salon* indeed, in which mixing furniture from periods—such as authentic pieces with modern chairs and armchairs—was the hallmark. *Plus ça change et plus c'est la même chose!*

On the other hand, in the houses of the *petit* bourgeois, whose social circle was almost exclusively limited to family members, the *salon* was not often used. If you were lucky enough to be able to afford one, it remained shrouded most of the year with protective covers (or *houses*), ghostly-looking sheets that made the *salon* appear like a forbidden land. The *petit salon* was where the action was, and often the room was used for reading and doing needlework. This smaller-scaled room had a cozier feeling, especially with its often worn chairs. By extension, "salon" became the appellation for the furniture used in a drawing room, being the key element of the room. Today's *salon* is the living room.

Chic Advice

A successful *salon,* or living room, needs a focal point. A mantel is best but if one is not available or possible, use something else, such as a huge mirror, a painting, or a view.

- It is important to hang pictures on the walls. Empty walls are sad-looking.

- Carpets are important—they create a feeling of warmth.

- Do not have too many leggy pieces of furniture in the room. Rule of thumb: one-third with legs, two-thirds with no legs.

- Light is always important, neither too much nor too little.

- Comfort is key. Always mix high and low, expensive, and less so. Be personal.

THE SOPHISTICATED SOFA

Thus first necessity invented stools. Convenience next suggested elbow-chairs. And luxury the accomplished Sofa last. —William Cowper (1731–1800). The sofa, as Cowper says, is an essential element of any *salon*. The word "sofa" is of Eastern origin and was first used in France around 1680 to designate a divan-like seat.

Upholstery, like so many elements in home decoration, is not new. Even the Egyptians, then, later, the Greeks and the Romans, upholstered their seats. They all had to sit somewhere. However, upholstery was fairly rudimentary in those times: Textiles or leather were stretched on a rigid framework. This fashion continued well into the Renaissance when saddlers were in charge of the arrangement for seats. Soon they all started to think that it was a bit hard on the behind and something had to be done about it.

At first it was quite simple. Quilted leather and stitching forming a lozenge pattern seems to have been favored in Spain and Italy before 1600. But by the beginning of the seventeenth century, a better solution began to be developed. Gradually, padding was made more comfortable by increasing the depth of the cushions and filling them with better materials: down, horsehair, soft feathers. The padding of the seat was laid on a lattice of webbing nailed across the seat-frame (exactly as it is on many chairs today). Shortly thereafter springs came into use, and, with this improvement, modern upholstery begins.

It was around 1740 that for the first time upholstery was studied in relation with the human body, and comfort was obtained from elaborate padding with horsehair, waste silk, and wool. It was about time! In all fairness, eighteenth-century chairs, especially French ones, are incredibly refined. It was quite a process. When the *menuisier*, followed by the sculptor and the *peintre doreur*, had finally completed the frame of a chair or a sofa, it was handed over to the *tapissier* (upholsterer) to work his magic. Great pains were taken to see that the material used was appropriate both to the frame and the setting for which it was intended. Even the smallest details, such as the braid and the gilded nails with which the upholstery was attached, were chosen with the greatest care so as to produce a harmonious effect. The English furniture

A watercolor drawing of an armchair by the French ornamental designer Richard de Lalonde (1782–86). Several of Lalonde's designs are identifiable from the seats made by Jacob Frères, Sené, and Delanois, all major eighteenth-century makers. Such watercolors, which were made to offer clients a variety of selections for the upholstery of their seating, provide an interesting view of late eighteenth-century Parisian taste.

designer Thomas Chippendale (1718–98) provides in his 1754 manual *The Gentlemen and Cabinet-Maker's Director* recommendations for upholstering chairs he made. Such details were important to him.

Very few antique seats retain their original upholstery, and when they do, it is often in a sad state of decay. So it is hard to imagine the beauty and sophistication of what was originally made. However, seats in the eighteenth century were quite sumptuous, and the upholsterer deserves at least as much credit as the carver or the sculptor for their finished appearance. Many upholsterers became rich and famous such as Simon de Lobel, the principal upholsterer to Louis XIV, or Capin, the royal *tapissier* during the time of Louis XVI (who managed to keep his head!).

A huge variety of fabric was used even then—from silk, patterned and striped, to velvets, stamped or plain; damask; leather; mohair; cotton, printed or not; and even *tapisserie*. However, *tapisseries*, such as Aubusson, Beauvais, and Gobelins, were employed less than we have been led to believe. Many older pieces of furniture were reupholstered with *tapisserie* in the nineteenth century. Upholstery was often enriched with tassels, trims, fringes, and cords. A braid or a fringe served the purpose of masking the bare joints and seams where the material was tacked down to the wooden framework. But fringe, especially in the nineteenth century, was also used purely for decoration. Indeed, the making of fringes has been described as one of the "ordinary pastimes" of ladies of this period. *Pourquoi pas?*

TOP: A watercolor drawing of a Louis XVI armchair by the French ornamental designer Richard de Lalonde (1782–86).

LEFT: A nineteenth-century drawing of an armchair, used by makers and upholsterers to provide options for their clients.

OPPOSITE: A detail of the sofa in the purple garden room—a simple duck cotton covered piece from Crate & Barrel. My friend, the painter Elizabeth Thompson, personalized it with large passionflowers, making it very special.

When not in use, expensively covered chairs were protected against dust and light by loose covers of a less pricey material, often serge, bay, cotton, or even taffeta. This practice seems to have lingered on almost until today—except that in some cases the process might be reversed, so that it is the slip-over covering that is made of the expensive fabric while the cheaper one remains fixed to the seat.

The twentieth century saw an increase in upholstered seats due to the rise of the middle class, and consequently the demand for comfort by a larger segment of the population. For many in the Western world, everyday life improved throughout the postwar era. Comfort has become synonymous with quality of life and lounging on a comfortable sofa watching television or entertaining friends has even become an expected part of that life.

No living room nowadays is complete without one or even several sofas, or *canapés*. Sadly, the term "couch potato" has even become part of the day-to-day vocabulary. Modern chemistry has produced new materials, and other innovations in upholstery have emerged as well. Down-like foam is often used and sometimes replaces springs, hair, and feathers. In some instances, new materials are employed with some form of the old spring and hair construction or with suspension springs or slats. Each of these has its champion. Modern science has increased the available construction alternatives.

Today, numerous houseware catalogues, from Calico Corners to Crate & Barrel or Pottery Barn, offer a wide range of classic and less traditional sofas and chairs placed together in a traditional fashion. They use steel coils tied together, often in eight directions, to create a uniform support for each frame. Spring down cushions,

in various degrees of firmness (extra firm, soft blend down, or hypo-allergenic) are standard on most frames. Striving for perfection, a manufacturer will use foam, feather, hair, latex, and springs, each for the job it does best, in a single sofa.

The old upholstery technique created at the end of the seventeenth century is still basically the same, only more refined as a result of modern technology. Changing habits rendered upholstery simpler, more foolproof, and no doubt more hygienic, too. However, it is still doubtful that the new foams will stand up to wear with the best of traditional upholstery. During the postwar era the use of latex or foam spread from automobile upholstery to the home, often as loose cushions over cable springs and, later, rubber webbing. The foam cushions do not hold up to the march of time well. The classic way of upholstering is still the best. The debt owed to Simon de Lobel, Louis XIV's principal *tapissier*, is immense.

Chic Advice

It is possible to buy a great sofa at Crate & Barrel. Either personalize it, like I did in my garden room, with hand-painted decoration or mix it with elegant accessories, as in my pool house. Remember the art of high and low. You can also splurge and have it custom-made. If you do this, try a moderate-priced fabric to keep the cost down.

A good trick for checking the quality of a sofa: Try to lift it by yourself; if you cannot do it, that's a good sign. Also, sit on the sofa before ordering it. When you find a shape that you like, you can reupholster a sofa many times over. Just remember that you need about 20 yards for a normal-sized sofa, so the fabric and labor can add up.

As Marie Antoinette was being sped through the cobblestone streets of Paris toward the Place de la Concorde to her miserable end, Revolutionary guards were busy compiling an inventory of her belongings. What they discovered among the expected heaps of ball gowns, baubles, and fine-crafted furniture were a few painted *jardinières*—trays and objects composed of tin. That such humble objects had fallen into such sophisticated hands testified to the extraordinary popularity of *tôle peinte*, a technique developed in the seventeenth century for finishing utilitarian metal goods. It is also a demonstration of the beloved mix of high and low—one of the staples of French style.

Originally a poor man's decoration, of the same ilk as today's mugs, snow globes, and other airport ephemera, *tôle* quickly shot up in status thanks to its ornamental appeal. Trays finished with a glossy layer of varnish like paint became a convincing and affordable knockoff of Oriental lacquer. Artists, occasionally even accomplished ones, brushed landscapes across planters mounted on lion's-paw feet. Classical acanthus leaf borders, often achieved by dipping a carved potato into paint, wound around everyday coffeepots and urns, shaped like their ancient Greek counterparts. Despite the French name, the first factories for

producing such wares were founded in England, in Bilston in Straffordshire, and most notably at Pontypool, in the south of Wales. In about 1660, Thomas Allgood (with such a name, the goods were bound to be good!) discovered a coal byproduct that could be made to adhere to metal by the application of heat, thus providing a firm surface that held thin coats of color. His secrets were passed on to his sons, and the business was so profitable that jealousy split Allgood's grandchildren, two of whom formed a rival company at Usk, in Wales. Both factories flourished throughout the eighteenth century, their products becoming so ubiquitous that expressions such as "round as a Pontypool waiter," were used to refer to both a large oval tray and a roly-poly person, came into general use.

A fine eighteenth-century *tôle* tray with a Neoclassical medallion in the center. To highlight its beauty, the tray is usually placed on the pool house *salon's* ottoman.

Both centers produced pieces of fine quality and both decorated them with flowers, fruits, berries, and birds, on brown, tortoiseshell, and black backgrounds. Some trays, circular, oval, octagonal, or rectangular, were real works of art brilliantly decorated by renowned painters, representing still lifes, historical or mythological scenes, landscapes, portraits, or *allégories*. The variety of decoration was endless as was the growing demand.

Different kinds of metal were japanned—bronze, copper, and even silver—but local sheet iron, covered with a layer of tin, was the most common base. Such success inspired other countries to test their own metal. Russian *tôle*, first made in the early 1700s in the Ural Mountains, is celebrated for its folksy flowers and high-keyed palette. German-speaking countries decorated tin ware with the same tulips and hearts that they sewed onto their quilts. These stylized motifs traveled to America with the Germans who settled in Pennsylvania. Fond as they were of lacquer, the French did not take up *tôle peinte* until the early 1760s, when they began to manufacture candelabra and other adornments for

mantels. Making up for a slow start, they produced an astonishing array of *tôle* objects over the next sixty years, ranging from watering cans painted with honeysuckle springs, to portly pear-shaped chocolate urns bearing gilded pagodas, to cache pots and urns. Most French *tôle* was made on a base of tin or iron. The colors were more vivid than those in England (but, of course!) and were finished with a coat of linseed oil, which produced a more brilliant surface but unfortunately caused crackling over the passage of time. In fact, quite a good effect!

The town of Dunkerque became renowned for the variety and range of *tôle* products. Overshadowed by the electroplating process, which revolutionized metal ware in the 1840s, *tôle* production eventually petered out. Today, however, thanks to the rage for painted finishes, vintage *tôle* is more prized than ever. Frequently found at antiques shops, *tôle* also turns up at auction. Prices range from $5 to $50 for a small repainted tray to well into five figures for an unusually elaborate table. Like all antiques, *tôle* is most desirable if left untouched. Rust, crackling paint, and dents, after all, are part of the charm.

Chic Advice

The care of painted metal is much the same as for painted wood. With all *tôle* ware the main danger is from rust, which may attack iron and steel once the surface has been chipped away. If used for table service, trays of *tôle peinte* should be protected from heat. Wet objects and spills need to be cleaned immediately in order to avoid ugly ring marks. Serious rusting on an antique piece should be referred to a restorer. On all other pieces do as I do and repaint it yourself. *Pourquoi pas?* French chic is all in the mix.

OPPOSITE, CLOCKWISE FROM TOP LEFT: An example of one of my cheap-chic dark green trays with chocolates on mini glass cake stands and flowers.

Another simple flea market *tôle* tray with dark green ivy-patterned decoration against a white background, echoing the floor stenciling.

A simple white-and-green *tôle* tray white—a thrift shop discovery—is instantly enlivened with green plastic glasses and a hand-painted ice bucket that is filled with fresh mint from the garden.

An assortment of *tôle* trays of various shapes purchased in flea markets and thrift shops have been spray-painted the same dark green. These inexpensive trays are an elegant way to present *hors d'oeuvres*.

The Billiard Room

Le château de construction moderne se déployait au bas d'une immense pelouse.
Le marquis s'avança et, offrant son bras a la femme du médecin, l'introduisit dans le vestibule.
En face montait un escalier droit . . . conduisait à droite sur le billiard,
dont on entendait, dès la porte caramboler les boules d'ivoire.

(The castle, a modern construction, was set at the bottom of a gigantic lawn.
The marquis came out and offered his arm to the doctor's wife, introducing her
in the entrance hall. Straight up was a staircase . . . which on its right opened
on the billiard room. Getting closer we could hear the noise of the ivory balls.

—Gustave Flaubert (1821–80), *Madame Bovary,* 1857

ALL RESPECTABLE FRENCH CHATEAUX, or country houses, had *une salle de billiard* (billiard room) in the nineteenth century. They still do. It was a way of entertaining yourself and your guests at the time—a wonderful social *passe-temps*. It still is.

The name "billiard" comes from the French (but of course, once again!) as a derivative of *bille* or *boulle*, the name of the ball initially used for the game. The game itself evolved from a lawn game similar to croquet, played as early as the eleventh century, called *jeu de Maille*. This early croquet-like game eventually led to the development of the *carom* or *carambole* billiards, which is played on a table without pockets.

The first recorded billiard set in royal inventories was ordered by Louis X of France in 1470. The game was played indoors on a wooden table covered with green cloth, to better simulate grass. A simple border was placed around the edges. The balls were shoved, rather than struck, with wooden sticks called *maces*, which looked very much like modern hockey sticks with blades. At first, the game was played with two balls on a table, which had six pockets and hoops similar to a croquet wicket. An upright stick was used as a target.

Since its start in the fifteenth century, billiards has had a long, rich, and varied history. It is a bit gory at first: The headless body of Mary, Queen of Scots, is rumored to have been wrapped in her billiard-table cover in 1586. *La pauvre.* The game was familiar enough among a large part of the population for Shakespeare to insert a mention of it into his play *Anthony and Cleopatra*, of 1609. The old girl, Cleopatra, utters these words: *Let us to billiards.*

On a lighter note, Louis XIV had an elaborate billiard room at Versailles, illuminated with twenty-six chandeliers and sixteen floor candelabras. Gambling and games were taken very

Many fun hours are spent in the billiard room. It is useful to have seats or a banquette for family and friends to relax while enjoying the game.

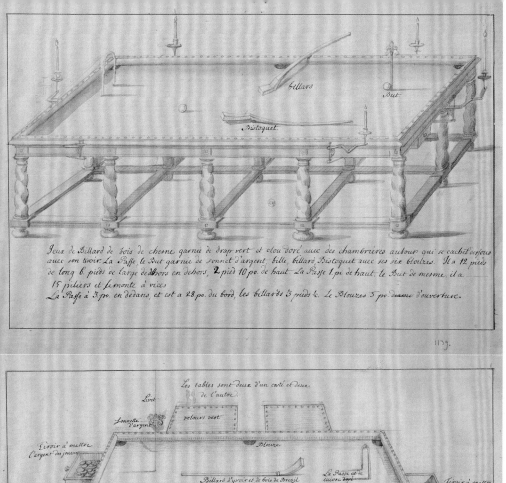

Jeux de Billard de bois de chesne garnie de drap vert et clou doré auec des chambrieres autour qui se cache serieus auec son tiroir. La Passe, le But garnie de sonnet d'argent, bille, billard, Bistoquet auec ses six blouzes. Il a 12 pieds de long 6 pieds de large de dehors en dehors, 2 pied 10 po. de haut. La Passe 1 pi de haut. le But de mesme. il a 15 piliers et se monte à vices.
La Passe à 3 po. en dedans, et est a 28 po. du bord, les billards 3 pieds ½. Le Blouzes 5 po. d'ouverture.

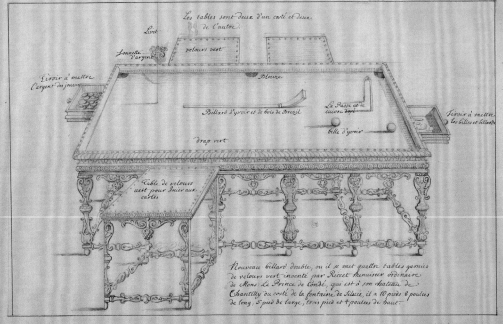

TOP: Drawing of a late-seventeenth-century French billiard table covered with green cloth and fitted with bells that rang when the post was struck. National Museum, Stockholm. Tessin Collection.

ABOVE: Drawing of a late-seventeenth-century French billiard table covered in green velvet, with a card table in front. This table was made for the Prince de Condé's Château de Chantilly. National Museum, Stockholm. Tessin Collection.

seriously indeed at court. From 1678 to the end of his reign, the *grands appartements du roi* served as the venue for the king's thrice-weekly evening receptions, known as *les soirées de l'appartement*. For these parties the rooms assumed specific functions. Food and drinks were served in the Salon de Venus where buffet tables were arranged; the Salon de Diane was transformed into a billiard room; dancing was in the Salon de Mars, which functioned as a ballroom; the Salon de Mercure became the gambling den or card room, and the Salon d'Apollon served as a music room. The Salon de Diane originally functioned as the west landing of the ambassador's staircase and formed the main entrance to the *grands appartements du roi*. It shows just how prominent billiards was at Versailles.

Speaking about American and French rapprochement, Washington and Lafayette often played billiards together, as a form of relaxation. Billiards was very much appreciated by many of America's founding fathers. Thomas Jefferson was so fond of the game that he concealed a billiard room in the dome of Monticello. Playing billiards was illegal in Virginia at that time; Jefferson's table was smuggled in among all the crates he brought back from his time in Paris. John Quincy Adams installed a billiard table at the White House in the presidential quarters and had to hear congressional criticism about his "gambling furniture." Abraham Lincoln raved about the game, calling billiards *health inspiring, scientific, and lending recreation to an otherwise fatigued mind.*

There are many sizes and styles of billiard tables. As a rule of thumb, tables are twice as long as they are wide and of rectangular shape. Most billiard tables are known as seven-, eight-, or nine-footers, referring to the table's long side. Pool halls tend to have eight-or nine-foot tables, as they cater to the serious pool shark. Remember Jackie Gleason and Paul Newman in *The Hustler*? They certainly made money playing pool—just don't try that at home! A billiard table will definitely ensure hours of fun for you, your kids, and your friends. *Amusez-vous bien.* But if the cues frighten you, watch a movie. A private home theater is the ultimate luxury—Louis XIV would have loved it. As a matter of fact, he built a lovely theater at Versailles.

Chic Advice

Try to choose an antique billiard table. It looks so much better than a contemporary one. An antique table is a good investment and has good resale value.

When deciding on the size of your table, don't forget that you need at least a two-foot clearance on all sides for the cues (billiard sticks).

Billiard cloths come in a large variety of colors. However, they have traditionally been green since at least the sixteenth century. Green is the easiest color for the eye, so stick to green.

It is good idea to have a bench for spectators in the billiard room.

If you build a private screening room, make it very cozy and comfortable. Splurge all the way. It is the ultimate luxury—always a high ticket when you sell your house. So, go for it.

A cover for a billiard table is a good idea, especially if the sun is strong in the room. It will protect the felt from fading.

The Library

Ma librairie est des belles entre les librairies de village.

(My library is a beauty among village libraries.)

—Michel de Montaigne (1532–92), from *Essays* (III: 3)

MONTAIGNE, A GREAT READER, philosopher, and writer, adored his *bibliothèque*, his library. It was without doubt his favorite spot in his château, one where he spent countless hours among his dear friends, *les livres*. Books for him became the companion of choice. The library, for the lucky people who could afford one, became the ideal place for retreat, study, daydreaming, or meditation. Montaigne wrote lovingly about his cherished place. First, the library was a retreat from the world. He emphasizes in his *Essays* its role as a refuge,

despite the fact that his was located on the top of a tower and exposed to the elements: *Chez moi je me trouve le plus souvent dans ma librairie.* (At home, I find myself often in my library.) The terms Montaigne uses to describe his *librairie* suggest a position of mastery. Its location allowed him a clear and immediate view of his surroundings and his books. *Je suis sur l'entrée.* At one sweep, he could command a view of his household. It was a round library. Who hasn't dreamed of a round library atop a tower? It is dreamy and romantic, conducive to intellectual forays. From such a perch, Montaigne could exert authority over all society, conjugal, filial, and civil: *C'est la mon siège.* (There is my throne.) The library became a command center of sorts, a source of creativity and nourishment. So it continued to be for intellectuals, writers, poets, philosophers, or mere *gens de lettres,* for centuries to come.

OPPOSITE: Organized and orderly books on the library bookshelves make it easier to locate what you are looking for.

RIGHT: The cover of *Les Aventures de Becassine*, a popular French comic book figure, from my father's collection.

A comfortable library needs good chairs, sofas, and light. Chairs, like this French Louis XV miniature *bergère*, can be adapted for young readers to make them feel welcome. A television is an entertaining addition. And what is more soothing than a green couch? Apple green is indeed the easiest color to live with.

159

By the end of the sixteenth century, the circulation of books increased. In 1701, 178 booksellers existed in Paris; thirty-six of them were printers and publishers. Libraries, old and new, were making their treasures more widely available. Royal edicts contributed to the new book mania. In 1617, Louis XIII ordered that two copies of every new publication in France be given to the Bibliothèque Royale (now Bibliothèque Nationale), in Paris. By 1622, their collection had 6,000 volumes; by 1715, largely through the zeal of Colbert (Louis XIV's capable minister), it grew to 70,000. This was due in part to Mazarin, who in 1661 bequeathed his rare library of 40,000 volumes to Louis XIV and France.

At the beginning of the sixteenth century, when books were rare and *très chers*, they were stored with great care in large chests, following the custom in the Middle Ages of storing anything valuable in a strongbox, which could be moved in case of emergency. As libraries grew, as numbers of books were printed, and the literacy rate increased, a more efficient way of storing books became necessary. The bookcase was born. At the beginning, protecting books from dust or rats seems to have been a great

ABOVE: A collection of leather-bound French books, including such classics as Jean-Baptiste Charcot's *Dans la Mer du Groenland*, accounts of his expeditions in Greenland, and works by Jules Verne.

OPPOSITE: Another practical touch to a library is a card table, making any card or board game possible—from Scrabble to bridge or Monopoly.

concern. The early *bibliothèque* had doors that hid the precious *livres* in closets. This was the case with the library of the Hôtel de Lauzun, with its 660 closets that had doors in the richly painted and decorated paneling. Then, during the seventeenth century, books started to be displayed. Drawings show built-in book cupboards in the *petite bibliothèque* of the Palais Royal, the shelves of which are fitted with dust-pelmets! The concern for dust must have been quite real in those large châteaux. A dust pelmet was not a bad idea, when you think about it!

During the time of François I, bookbinding was considered a special art. When books started to be displayed in a bookcase, bookbinding became even more important. The cover of the book not only had elaborate ornaments but the edges were gilded and tooled, even painted. We can only marvel at the excellence of the material and careful workmanship in well-preserved bindings—even the color of the leather is in perfect condition. Morocco and calf were the leathers that were primarily used from the seventeenth century on, the latter preferred for its softness, smooth surface, and receptivity to design.

Soon satirical prints and *gazettes* mocked the taste of scholars or members of the nobility for handsome bindings. In one instance a verse reads: *C'est bien le plus grand fou qui soit dans la nature qui se plaist aux livres bien dorez, bien couvers, bien reliés, bien nets, bien epoustez, et ne les voit jamais que par la couverture.* (The greatest of all nature's fool is he who likes his books all gilt, well covered, well bound, nice and clean and dust free, and who never looks at anything but the cover.)

As with all caricatures, some truth lies behind this one, as sometimes books were bought for the color and texture of their binding as well as for their contents. The bibliophile's relation to books was often sensuous and involved more than just the text. But serious writers and readers—like Voltaire for example—were buying bound books with only a paper cover. The first task was to add in the corrections from the errata sheet. The second task was to send the volume to a bookbinder to have it recovered in the leather of choice, morocco or calf leather, and then brand a bookplate on its cover, usually a coat of arms, providing that you had one.

As with so many things having to do with design, book display was codified too. Under Louis XV, a classical arrangement of books was organized by decreasing size, with folio editions on the lowest shelves and the smallest formats—12 and 16 centimeters—on top. *Somptuosité* turned into luxury and libraries provided real

Chic Advice

- When cleaning your books, be aware of dust and mice.
- The best woods from which to build your bookcase are pine (soft and easy to work with), ash, maple (very good to work with, and can be stained in many colors), cherry wood (very good and very expensive), and mahogany (very good and very expensive).
- Read all your books. Do not have them for display only.
- The best way to save money on bookcases is to use painted or stained wood.
- Always try to have a comfortable sofa and good lighting in a library.
- A hidden television in a cabinet is a good option as well as a table for a game, quick tea, or dinner. It could be a skirted table—a good way to mix high and low.

comfort. Readers could daydream and loll on carved and painted *duchesse* or *duchesse en bâteau*. Life was good. The *fauteuil de bureau* supported in style the busy writer at his desk—usually a *bureau plat*—and files were tucked away in a *cartonnier*. Library steps were a very functional addition to many *bibliothèques*, and globes, normally in pairs—one terrestrial and one celestial—were in great demand. Special lighting, such as massive *torchères* or candles, were required if people wanted to read or write after dark, which they did quite often. Candles served a dual purpose, being useful also for melting sealing wax.

By the end of the sixteenth century, studies and libraries had become not only places to read and write; they were depositories of rarities, a

A well-appointed library needs to have a good bar in the corner. Mine is a mixture of crystal and glass; a glass decanter stands guard. The antique chest has ample depth to hold and hide the various bottles.

sort of *cabinet de curiosité* holding all kinds of marvels, from ostrich eggs to precious stones. Private libraries grew even larger. Voltaire, for example, had in his possession as many as 7,500 volumes. Quite a number! By its very composition, his *bibliothèque* offers us a model for the collection of a savant, *encyclopédiste* of the eighteenth century. Works of philosophy and law, which Voltaire used successfully in his battle with the Catholic Church, are prominently featured in addition to books related to world history, the history of France, and physics. On his shelves, Voltaire had Latin authors, sometimes in the original and sometimes in French translation, including Petronius, Virgil, Cicero, Juvenal, Ovid, and Horace. There were also French authors such as La Fontaine, Montaigne, and Bossuet, in addition to Voltaire's own writings.

Books were a luxury indeed and on occasion quite valuable. They were a source of knowledge, information, and entertainment, as well as a display of intellectual curiosity—as they are today. Books and libraries are to be cherished, even more so in our computer age. They enhance our lives and transport us in another universe. Their presence will make your home more personal, too. *J'aime les livres, beaucoup, passionement, à la folie!*

The Dining Room

La salle à manger est un théâtre,
dont la cuisine est la coulisse et la table, la scène.
(The dining room is a theater, the kitchen
functions as backstage, and the table as the scene.)
—Chatillon-Plessis, 1894

THE FRENCH TERM *salle à manger* (dining room) was not coined until late in the eighteenth century, but rooms labeled as such were reported to exist prior to that time. For example, when the ambassadors from Siam visited Paris and Versailles in 1686, they were provided with an *appartement*, which included a *salle à manger*. Madame de Montespan, King Louis XIV's mistress, also had in her Château de Clagny, which was a marvel of luxury and done to the latest fashion, *une salle à manger*.

Frenchmen and women tended to dine ceremonially in the *salle* and less formally in a *sallette* (which means "small room"). As extra rooms, notably the *antichambre*, were interposed between the *salle* and the *chambre*, it was often in one of these new rooms that the family dined. The *première antichambre du roi* at Versailles was also known as the *salle où le roi mange* or the *salle du grand couvert*.

In the seventeenth century more than one room was used for dining. The location of a meal changed depending on the number of guests, their social rank, the occasion, or even the season. The table was never left standing in the middle of a room before or after the meal. So, dining tables, which are tables used primarily for meals, are a relatively modern invention, as is the dining room itself.

In the Middle Ages, tables used for meals varied immensely in size and form according to the position they were intended to occupy. The dining tables of the great hall, where it was customary for the members of the whole household to assemble and take their meals, were in fact massive boards of oak or elm resting on a series of trestles. Banquets were the recognized form of hospitality. The amount of food served on these occasions was stupendous. Chicken, goats, oxen, and mutton by the thousands were killed and prepared,

OPPOSITE: *La table est mise.* The table is set; silverware and china are out. We are ready for a party. The top plates are rare 1846 Sèvres porcelain from the Château des Tuileries, which I found a couple of years ago by chance at an auction here in America. They have a vivid blue border with hand-painted angels holding the royal crest and initial.

OVERLEAF: The table shines and glitters with an abundance of colors of the china, silver, and flowers. The mood is certainly festive. The sideboard displays candles in silver candleholders. A pretty French porcelain bowl full of fresh fruit is at the ready for dessert. The stage is set. On the walls are eighteenth-century French wallpaper panels in the Neoclassical style after Hubert Robert.

gargantuan amounts of sweets were piled up, fantastic sugar confections passed around, bread of all types was sliced by the bread "trenchers" (a real job, by the way). Different qualities of breads were served according to the rank of the person, with the upper crust reserved for lords only—hence the expression! For all of that tables of great length and strength were required. The tops were detachable and the entire table was frequently removed after meals, sometimes to make space for dancing. Talk about a cozy little get-together! On these occasions, the high table for the master and most important guests stood on the dais under a canopy, while at right angles to it, down the length of the hall, side tables were placed for the remainder of the company.

For smaller gatherings, documented in illuminated manuscripts of the fourteenth and fifteenth centuries, small tables, which could be drawn up to the fire in winter (very important—imagine the drafts in these places!) are generally portrayed with shaped ends but were sometimes round. These tables would have served many purposes. The versatile round table was used by the Egyptians, and the Greeks had small tables that were similar. Usually a table for each person was placed beside the couch on which that person reclined while eating—quite similar to the TV tables of modern-day couch potatoes. Needless to say, these Greek tables survived in ancient Rome where they were often created with elaborate wrought legs.

The use of a single large communal dining table seems to have derived from the practice of Northern European barbarians and the Vikings. The practice of using trestle tables continued well into

The white tablecloth makes the table sing by creating a crisp backdrop. The plates are a mixture of different patterns, playing on variations of white and gold. The *mélange* gives a more personal look. If you do not have complete sets, remember that mixing is very chic. The flowers in the middle are low and unobtrusive allowing guests to see one another from across the table, which is essential for a convivial meal. A few petals have been spread around the middle for a more fanciful look. This is a very easy decorative touch. Candy in little crystal cups, as well as the striped candles, add a touch of color.

the seventeenth century during which their instability must have occasioned many accidents. Perhaps to counterbalance such unhappy events, expanding tables started to appear in France during the sixteenth century. However, as noted, it was rare to have a special room dedicated to eating meals.

By the seventeenth century, the medieval eating habits, such as passing spoons and knives from person to person, were fading away. A strong emphasis was placed on cleanliness in the kitchen—still a far cry from today's standards—and stricter table manners emerged. *Service à la française*, or French service, was an orchestrated ritual that dictated with absolute precision the order in which the various courses were served and the symmetrical arrangement on the table of the dishes that composed each course. The dinner plates lined the edges of the table and serving dishes occupied its center in a prearranged pattern. Even the size of the *assiette* (plate) was codified: large ones were 16 ⅕ inches in diameter, medium ones 15 inches, and small ones 12 inches.

As a matter of fact, Louis XIV is recorded as personally checking the table plan for many of his important banquets. A rehearsal was often suggested. A classical banquet of *service à la française*, under the reign of the Sun King was like a Chinese buffet, with many dishes to share at each course. It was so costly that such banquets were given only in grand houses on important occasions. They were divided into three parts: The first service covered the menu from the soup to the roast, including the *hors-d'oeuvre*, the second from the roast and vegetables to the sweet dishes, and the third consisted of pastries, *petits fours,* ices, and fruits. A dazzling display of silverware, candelabra, and flowers completed the effect. Immaculate, starched linen damask, or rich *indiennes* tablecloths covered these elaborate tables, enhanced with assorted napkins. Their size was also regulated: 70 to 100 centimeters in the seventeenth century. Another *forté* of the French was folding napkins. Many manuals of the period provided up to twenty-seven ways of presenting them, in shapes resembling birds, animals, or fruits. Glasses did not usually sit on the table but on a sideboard in a *rafraichissoir,* to keep cool. Wine, when needed, was brought over by servants and diluted with water.

To create a festive mood, china and crystal glasses play on a symphony of yellow and red. Candleholders filled with orange candles have been added for an extra zest of color.

Beauty is in the details. So is whimsy, as in the case of these snail-shaped place-card holders.

We had to wait until after the French Revolution to finally see the stationary table become the center of attention in the dining room. Intimate suppers became the height of fashion, provided the company was homogenous. For these new private dining rooms, the shape of the table had to be modified. Round or oval tables made in sections with legs and supports became the norm, as well as did central pedestals. A new wood—mahogany—was also introduced at the time; it was strong but less heavy and easier to work with than oak. The fashion spread rapidly to all the other European countries and to America. A more informal setting for dinner led to a simplified service.

Service à la russe, or Russian service, was introduced to high society by the Prince Kourakine, the tsar's ambassador to Paris during the Second Empire. Hence the name from where it spread throughout the eating world. The aim was to have hot dishes as hot as possible instead of leaving guests to choose from a variety of dishes that were more likely to get cold. The serving order was organized in advance so that the dishes would not lose their flavor. Dishes were served from the left of a seated person, and the plates were taken away or put down from the right. The same principles are still followed today. The table was set with *assiettes*. The name derives from the fact that it marked the position of the eater at the table, where he or she was seated (*assis*). Etiquette requires that two similar-sized plates never be placed on top of each other. However, changing plates is necessary after the fish course and for the cheese course. Rules and regulations continued to dictate table setting. In 1890 *Le Dictionnaire de la vie practique* announced that the space between each *assiette* had to be between 12 to 16 inches. For the first time, in the nineteenth century, glasses were part of the table display, yet their appearance was also strictly regulated. For a carefully prepared meal three matching glasses were placed left to right in decreasing size, for water, for white wine, and for red wine. The set was sometimes completed with a flute or cup if the meal was to end with champagne. What a display! Poets have celebrated the beauty of wine and its container, including Rémi Belleau (1528–77): *Crystal hante mignardement, Sur un pied qui fait justement, La base d'une colonette* (Crystal delicately poised, On a stem which in fact is like, The base of a little column.)

The tablecloth should be 16 inches away from the floor. The dining room floor itself should be made of parquet with a small *tapis* (rug) under the table. This was considered more hygienic. On a table the space allotted to each diner needed to be about two-and-half feet. No unnecessary squashing and flirting during the prudish nineteenth century! From that point on, the dining room, when utilized as intended, was a place of tremendous importance. Here, the family put itself on display for its guests, showing off its silver and precious crystal and china, exhibiting the centerpiece it had commissioned from a fashionable goldsmith, hanging portraits, and subdued wallpaper on the wall. Mealtime had moved to of the center of social intercourse. It was at the table that deals were done. It still is, especially in France! Ambition was avowed and marriages concluded. A place for social gatherings, the dining room was also the place where family members gathered daily. A meal was not just consumption of food but a family occasion as well. The homemaker's manuals all stressed the importance of the mistress of the house in creating an agreeable atmosphere as well as good food.

Gastronomic horizons expanded accordingly, and became a mark of prestige and a sign of excellence. Gourmet dining symbolized conquest and sophistication. It became a token of success and prosperity. In recent years, we have seen a return to the old-fashioned virtues of the dining room with all its trappings as a measure of social success alongside gourmet cooking. Private dinner parties at home are appreciated for their conviviality. However, the habit of our ancestors of varying the location of a meal at home, depending on the time of day, the number of guests, the occasion, or the season, was a good idea. I urge you to try it. It makes the meal more fun, and variety in life is always good. *A table, Madame est servie.*

Chic Advice

- The best dining tables are round as they are more democratic and conducive to conversation.

- An option to save money is an inexpensive table covered with a beautiful skirt.

- Comfortable and strong chairs are important. If you choose some from Crate & Barrel or a similar store, finish them with cushions or stencils.

- Sideboards can be bought at auction. They are now a good deal. Or, purchase a simple cabinet or side table.

- Invest in pretty china and glasses in a variety of patterns that you can mix to create a personal touch.

- Antique silver can be found at flea markets or at auction. Do not hesitate to mix and match styles or patterns.

LEFT: The pool house dining room's simple white Crate & Barrel wood chairs are enhanced with my dark green hand-stenciling. They complement the decoration of the white tree-trunk table that I designed, with its stenciled border along the edge of the surface. The tabletop setting is a variation of greens that is accentuated by playful orange and pink.

TOP: A French Sêvres plate designed by me. I sold them in my store in New York.

RIGHT: It is fun to set up tables in different spots and change them depending on the weather and the number of guests. Here, on the poolside table is a colorful mix of pottery in different shades of green and silver, with lime green plastic glasses.

THE FORK: A NEW DISCOVERY

Eat with your fingers. Our ancestors were doing it. The glorious Louis XIV, in spite of the strict etiquette that he established, ate with his fingers until the end of his life. His sister-in-law, the Princess Palatine, remarked that most of those who dined at the king's table used only their knives and fingers. You know the joke. Ask, "What's that?" Then, show both your hands and fingers. And say, "Ten pieces of Italian dinnerware!" But that is unfair; the Italians are the one who started the use of silverware. In the late eleventh century, when a Byzantine princess arrived in Venice to marry the Doge, it was found that she ate her food with a golden fork. She was reprimanded by the bishop for antisocial behavior—her unwillingness to share others' germs!

The fork came into general use only during the Renaissance, and only for lifting morsels onto one's own plate. European manners can be studied from the stream of manuals written to teach people how to behave. The earliest manuals, such as *De institutione novitarum* by Hugh St. Victor, of 1141, were addressed to clerics. The thirteenth-century *Bavarian Hofzucht (Courtly Manners)*, attributed to Tannhäuser, was directed at boorish courtiers, as was John Russell's fifteenth-century *Book of Courtesye*. The most influential publication of the genre, *De Civilitate Morum Puerilium* of 1530, by Erasmus, ran into 130 editions. It was reprinted in Russia when Peter the Great sought to civilize his court two hundred years later.

In medieval times, people served themselves from a common plate with their hands. Two or three

A good way to store silver is to keep it neatly in boxes with *chamois* so that it does not tarnish too fast.

people sipped soup from the same bowl. Bread and meat were dipped in the same salt cellars. The first forks were used for sweet foods (fruits in syrups, for example), mainly in Southern Europe. This type of fork, often carried together with a spoon and toothpick, was a personal object rather than one provided by a host for his guest, and was usually made with two prongs. A revolution in table manners came in the fifteenth century in Italy with the increasing substitution of a fork for the fingers in carrying food to the mouth (especially meat). At the time, knives, forks, and spoons were of brass, rarely of silver. From the sixteenth century on, the use of the fingers tended increasingly to be forbidden in most European countries.

It was Henri III of France who first introduced to the French the custom of using a two-pronged fork at the table, launching the habit among the nobility. He noted after visiting the Venetian court in 1574 that a two-pronged table fork was being used. It was a wise decision, considering the fashion of the time—high collars and ruffs! By the seventeenth century, every wealthy French aristocrat (the English a bit later) had his own plate, glass, knife, spoon, fork, napkin, and bread. Silver or silver gilt were the materials of choice. In order to prevent servants and indelicate guests from making off with the silverware, forks, spoons, and other utensils were engraved with the owner's initials or crest. Around 1660, napkins came into vogue, and marvel of marvel, guests were no longer expected to wipe their fingers on the tablecloth! By the eighteenth century, dining had become a complex ritual, and an occasion for social display. Eating in company required self-control; it became a type of ballet. The use of diverse utensils required intense training. For example, food was not to be placed in the mouth with the tip of

the knife. Spoons came in a bewildering variety of shapes: stew spoons, coffee spoons, spoons for *entremets,* and so on. You really had to learn which one to use if you wanted a place in society.

In the eighteenth century, forks took on the shape that we know today, but forks are so confusing. The French use a fork with the right hand (providing that they are right-handed) as a pick. Americans use it in the same hand but they often use it to convey food to the mouth. Then there is the complicated matter of the fish fork, meat fork, salad fork, and dessert fork. Which fork is for what? Meat necessitated forks that were simpler, stronger, and larger than those only for sweets, which are now called "suckets" forks. The first meat forks had two or three prongs but a four-pronged type was developed before the end of the seventeenth century and is still used today. During the nineteenth century, just as today, children were scolded by their parents for eating with their fingers. However, fast food, Big Macs, chicken nuggets, and French fries have made the use of the fork and spoon obsolete. Fingers are in fashion for the fast-food consumer! For others, silverware still prevails. For everyday use, cutlery is rarely made of precious metal; it is often made of cast aluminum (and does not require initials in order to keep thieves at bay). Silver plate is also popular for everyday use because it resists tarnish and acquires the warm patina of a prized heirloom. Today, engraved silverware handed down from beloved grandmothers or bought at a country auction adds immediate breeding to a dinner table. The rules and customs established in the eighteenth century still prevail, and a total lack of table manners is still a kiss of death in social circles. The well-known French phrase *Il ne sait même pas tenir une fourchette* (He doesn't even know how to hold a fork.) expresses this perfectly.

In 1846, E. Briffault ended his *Paris à Table* with this assessment: *The two-pronged fork is used in Northern Europe. The English are armed with steel tridents with ivory-handled three-pronged forks—but in France, we have the four-pronged fork, the height of civilization.* Today, a more relaxed social attitude allows a return to the "manners" of the Middle Ages such as dipping bread in olive oil. Who knows, perhaps in the twenty-second century, we will all use our fingers again!

I like colorful tables. It is a pleasure to mix several sets of dishes and patterns together depending on the occasion or the time of the year. Top each place setting with a consommé bowl (a more elegant way to serve soup than a traditional bowl).

The Kitchen

Lorsqu'il n y aura plus de cuisine dans le monde,
il n'y aura plus de lettres, d'intelligence elevée et rapide,
de relations liantes; il n'y aura plus d'unité sociale.

(When cooking disappears from the world,
it would be the end of literature, high and quick intelligence,
close relationships; it would mean the end of social unity.)

—Marie-Antoine Carême (1784–1833)

WE HAVE COME A LONG WAY. Can you imagine that for a long time cooking was done in separate buildings, and sometimes in the outdoors! In our large comfortable kitchens, microwave ovens—which I am not overly fond of—and computer-like stoves have given us speed and efficiency.

The ancients cooked as much as we do now and developed methods that showed genius and inspiration. In biblical times houses were designed around central courtyards, so cooking in the warm climate could be done out-of-doors. Meats were roasted on the original barbecue, camping style. This was done squatting in front of an open fire. Maybe we should try it next time! It is not easy to make a roast medium rare that way. Breads, which were a basic part of many diets, were baked in clay ovens. And the Greeks, who ate cakes of grain instead of bread, baked large, thin cakes on a plate of iron or a hot stone outside.

Until the thirteenth century, kitchens always seemed to be located in a separate building in the

OPPOSITE: At work in the kitchen cutting a lovely baguette on an essential piece of equipment—a wooden cutting board. A breadbox is another useful item.

RIGHT: Just outside the kitchen is the pantry. Painted a deep ocher yellow—a sunny *Provençale* color—it radiates with light, even on a gloomy day. Neatly organized canisters lining the walls are full of goodies, including *pâte de fruit*.

courtyard or garden. Nobody but the cook had to stand the heat of the fireplace in the middle of August. In subsequent centuries, when enough lords had their fill of eating cold food, kitchens were finally moved into the main house. But for a long time they were confined to garrets; the fear of fire was a real concern and so was the problem of smoke and cooking odors. Smelling food when you enter a great palace—how *déclassé!*

By the end of the sixteenth century, for convenience, kitchens were moved to the "noble floors." Finally, a hot meal! In order to make sure that the aroma of food did not linger in the large reception room, pantries, which were very handy for all sorts of storage—from fruits to jams, herbs, bread, and cheeses—were created to act as a buffer. The kitchens at this time were well stocked and often equipped with a great variety of objects that were more costly than those found in living rooms. Utensils of iron, copper, tin, terra-cotta, and wood were used for preparing meals and banquets. Bread bins, molds, and knives could be found on easily accessible shelves.

Good food put the master in good spirits, but even more, it became a means of ostentatious display, another *signe extérieur de richesse.* Progress in visual and culinary amenities was facilitated by improvements in the water supply to private houses. As much as possible, each house tried to have its own well, permitting water to be hoisted directly from a source in the ground. It was a great boon to hygiene, cleanliness, and cooking, as well as to thirsty lads. Meats and birds of all feathers were roasted in the kitchen's humongous fireplace; one of the numerous kitchen aides had the duty of spitting the meat. Water and liquids were kept hot once again by the flames of the hearth. Breads were baked in a special area in the fireplace.

LEFT: Teapots and a cookie jar decorate the kitchen corner shelves; their colors work well with the walls.

RIGHT: The large sunny kitchen boasts one of my favorite countertop materials— stainless steel. The wooden floor surface is easy on the feet. The wall is painted a typical French color, which is used extensively in the South of France, its lively shade like a ray of sunshine.

Following the fashion of earlier times, sometimes a special baking oven was built outside.

Kitchens were rustic by today's standards, but they were large, hospitable, and comfortable. Somehow, delicious food was created and French *cuisine* became the envy of all European courts. The word for kitchen in French is *cuisine*. It is interesting to note that it means the physical place as well as the food that is prepared. *Haute cuisine* became the appellation of great French cooking and its hallmark.

After 1600, gastronomical principles were introduced into the kitchen. Nicolas de Bonnefons wrote in his *Délices de la campagne* of 1654: *The subject of this third book is that true taste is to be given every food. It should be simple because it is called healthy. A cabbage soup should be flavored entirely with cabbage, a leek soup entirely with leeks.* Bonnefons, by the way, was the first to encourage aristocrats to cultivate their gardens. *Le potager du Roi* at Versailles, which had been recently re-created, was the

TOP: My collection of colorful pitchers above the refrigerator adds warmth and life to the already inviting kitchen.

ABOVE: Fresh herbs are essential ingredients for good cooking in my book. They instantly elevate simple preparations to a higher level.

OPPOSITE: The cozy corner banquette in the kitchen— the perfect spot for a quick breakfast of tea or coffee and croissants. *Bien sur!*

most famous. So by the end of the seventeenth century, cabbage, onions, and various kinds of roots began to appear on aristocratic tables as well as those of the lower classes. Asparagus, originally popular in the south of France, began to be grown in other parts of the country, and it was used in refined cooking. Young fresh vegetables became the rage. The Sun King lost his head over small green peas; it turned into a galloping passion. He adored them. The Marquise de Maintenon, rumored to be the

king's morganatic wife, described the court as being in a "frenzy" over peas!

In order to preserve the characteristic taste of such foods, chefs (*cuisiniers*) in aristocratic kitchens acquired the habit of cooking each ingredient of a complex dish separately. *Vous imaginez le travail!* Another technique of good chefs in the seventeenth and eighteenth centuries was to cook meat rather rare and serve it without sauce. In 1660, Pierre de Lune wrote in the *Nouveau Cuisinier*: *Ducks and waterfowls should be drained and roasted on a spit without larding and when half done they should be seared with lard and eaten quite rare, with salt and white pepper and orange juice or a natural poivrade.* Quick cooking was recommended not only for roasted meat but also for such vegetables as asparagus. *Le Cuisinier Français* warned in 1651: *Ne les faites pas trop cuire.* (Do not overcook them.) So much for the *nouvelle cuisine* of the last twenty years!

LEFT: In the largely green-and-white pool-house kitchen, the open shelves display colorful china. The plate rack above the antique sink creates a focal point that adds character to the space. The old-fashioned soapstone sink creates age and drama in the otherwise modern kitchen. The countertop is made of my other favorite material—concrete, stained a mossy green. Plants keep the kitchen in the pool house lively and enforce its green-and-white color scheme.

ABOVE: All chic kitchens should have a French stove. My dark green enamel Lacanche stove is enhanced with a wall of hand-painted tiles.

At the end of the seventeenth century, famous chefs had reached a level of celebrity that is now reserved for pop stars. Vatel, the *cuisinier* for the Prince de Conde, became a legend. He took so much pride in his accomplishments that rather than face dishonor, he preferred to kill himself after having failed to serve what he thought was an adequate meal to guests (I grant you they were royal guests), as the Marquise de Sevigné recounts in one of her letters to her daughter. Vatel may have overreacted a tad.

Food, cooking, cuisine, and *haute cuisine* were nothing to trifle with; they were the subject of many discussions and much important writing. In 1691, Massianot defended the culinary arts and the superior taste of the French. Voltaire in his *Dictionnaire philosophique* went a step farther and developed a parallel between good taste in food and good taste in literature and art, all of which were the prerogative of the French. *Bien sûr. Gastronomie* sprung to life after the Revolution in a world where many traditions had vanished. It became a link to the past, a continued source of Gallic pride.

Food literature abounded. Grimod de La Reynière led the way by publishing in 1804 the *Almanach des Gourmands*, a food guide that proved to be enormously successful. He famously said: *Méfiez-vous des gens qui ne mangent pas. Ils sont en general envieux, sots ou mechants. L'abstinence est une vertue antisocial.* (Be aware of people who are not eating. They are usually jealous, stupid, or nasty. Abstinence is an antisocial virtue.)

Brillat-Savarin, another legendary foodie, had the ambition to make culinary art a true science. He achieved his goal with the publication in 1825 of his *Physiologie du gout ou Médiations de gastronomie transcendante*. However, the one who really modified the culinary practice of his time was Carême, the pastry chef and *cuisinier* of Talleyrand and the Rothschilds, with his *L'art de la Cuisine au XIX siecle*. A recognized founder of French *haute cuisine*, his work raised him to the pinnacle of his profession. Carême had a keen sense of what was both fashionable and entertaining. So he prepared both spectacular and refined recipes. The *vol-au-vent* and large *meringues* are culinary creations attributed to him. Although an incomparable pastry chef, he was also famous for soups and sauces. In keeping with his serious culinary activities, Carême was also concerned with the arrangement of a *cuisine*. He redesigned certain kitchen utensils, changed the shape of saucepans, and designed new molds. At his death, the Russian tsar Alexander I (for whom he also worked) said to Talleyrand: *What we did not know was that he taught us to eat.*

Escoffier, hailed by all the best chefs as their master, taught quite a few how to eat too. Born in 1847, in the south of France near Cannes, he was twelve years old when he started to work in a kitchen with no

OPPOSITE, CLOCKWISE FROM TOP LEFT: Who could have breakfast without French croissants? Certainly not me! And tea, with of course a tea cozy!

I love tea in all its forms, so it is no surprise that I have an amusing collection of teapots.

If you feel up to making a French paté—a meat terrine—use a lovely decorative mold. It is much easier to prepare than you think.

electricity, no gas, no running hot or cold water, and none of the many labor-saving gadgets of today. A mayonnaise had to be made by hand—this was easy. Egg white for *meringues* had to beaten by hand—not so easy. As Escoffier once said: *One must not forget that good, sound cooking, even the very simplest, makes a contented home.* For Carême, as well as for Voltaire, *haute cuisine* transcends food, and being able to appreciate it is the manifestation of a sophisticated human being, who is both social and intellectual. More than a century later, the ritual of dining—breakfast, lunch, and dinner—that had once determined the tempo of family life was on the way out due to increased hours spent at work (especially for women). Meals in the second half of the twentieth century were prepared as quickly as they were consumed. Frozen and freeze-dried foods simplified life. New technology, including the microwave, came to the rescue. Instead, coffee, powdered milk, and instant soups became the rage. Everyone was pressed for time, and being busy, even overwhelmed, became almost a status symbol. Frozen food in the late 1950s was another boom; the age of the frozen dinner began in a totally compressed kitchen. Remember the kitchenette?

All of a sudden, the pendulum swung the other way and a yearning for natural, healthy, and delicious food returned. The pleasure of a good dinner is now more than ever appreciated by all. Today the old-fashioned kitchen is in vogue again, yet with all the modern amenities—dishwasher, freezer, and oven—putting the kitchen at the center of the family life once again. Good food, good company, and family in a warm kitchen are the best antidote once again in a difficult world. Today, the pantry is still in use, a delightful addition to a working kitchen. And often practical, hygienic, stainless steel is required following the lead of well-known chefs who loves stainless steel for its easy care. Unlike marble, stainless steel is nonporous and doesn't absorb bacteria. Many chefs think that hygiene is the future in kitchens—and so do I.

For a fleeting moment we thought we could survive without kitchens but we were wrong. They are the heart and soul of a home, with or without a fireplace in wood, marble, or stainless steel. It is just a question of personal taste.

Chic Advice

Kitchen Must-haves

- Natural light. A real luxury and an important element in making your kitchen user-friendly.

- Two dishwashers. They are also cheaper than having built-in cabinets.

- Two sinks: one deep enough to hide dirty pots, and one of normal depth.

- Hidden garbage receptacles. It helps having a clean-looking kitchen when the counters have built-in garbage chutes. Trash disposal receptacles can be hidden inside cabinets behind closed doors.

- My favorite kitchen counter is stainless steel, for hygienic reasons, or stained concrete.

- A French stove: either Lacanche or La Cornue.

- A butler's pantry or service pantry; once considered old-fashioned, it is back in style because of its practicality.

Chic Menus & Recipes

Menus

Chic Brunch à la Proust

Tomato Pie (Tarte à la tomate)

Zucchini Tian

Madeleines du coté de chez Proust

Chic Purple Delight Lunch

Beet Soup with Sour Cream and Fingerling Potatoes (Soupe de betteraves)

Clafoutis with Black Cherries comme à la maison

Chic Cliché Lunch à la Française

Chic Quiche

Grated Carrots with Vinaigrette Classique

Red Fruit Mousse with Raspberry Coulis and Fresh Mint

Chic Dinner aux Bougies

Arugula Salad with Chive Flowers and Vinaigrette Classique

Stuffed Rack of Veal

Zucchini Gratin

My Grandmother's Chocolate Cake (Gâteau au chocolat de ma grandmère)

Chic Brunch à la Proust

TOMATO PIE
(TARTE À LA TOMATE)

Serves 6

¼ teaspoon unsalted butter

One 9-inch store-bought pie crust

2 tablespoons Dijon mustard

½ pound Swiss cheese, grated

3 large tomatoes, sliced ¼-inch thick

⅓ teaspoon fresh thyme leaves, coarsely chopped

Coarse sea salt, a pinch

1 dozen fresh opal basil leaves, left whole

Butter a 9-inch ceramic pie dish. Place pie crust inside the dish. Spread mustard thinly on crust. Place cheese evenly over the mustard. Cover with tomato slices in a tightly packed single layer. Then sprinkle with thyme and salt.

Bake in a preheated 350°F. oven until crust is brown, about 45 minutes. Remove dish from oven. Set aside for 15 minutes. Sprinkle basil on top.

ZUCCHINI TIAN

Serves 6 to 8

2 tablespoons extra-virgin olive oil

2 large cloves garlic, peeled

2 sprigs fresh thyme

6 medium zucchini, about 1½ pounds, peeled and thinly sliced into rounds

3 cups cooked long-grain rice, cooled to room temperature

3 large eggs

1 cup heavy cream

1 cup grated Swiss cheese

Heat oil in a skillet over medium heat. Add garlic, 1 sprig of thyme, and zucchini. Sauté, stirring frequently until zucchini is tender, about 8 minutes. Remove pan from heat. Discard garlic and thyme. Set aside.

Place rice in a bowl. Mix in eggs, heavy cream, ¾ of cup grated cheese, remaining thyme, and zucchini. Spread mixture evenly in a 10-inch gratin dish. Sprinkle remaining cheese on top.

Bake in a preheated 350°F. oven until top is brown and crisp, about 20 to 25 minutes. Remove dish from oven. Set aside for 15 minutes. Serve warm or at room temperature.

MADELEINES DU COTÉ DE CHEZ PROUST

Makes about 2 dozen Madeleines

1 cup granulated sugar

4 eggs

1 teaspoon rum

1 cup all-purpose flour

1¼ sticks unsalted butter

1 tablespoon confectioner's sugar

In a small bowl, combine the sugar and eggs. Stir in the rum. Add flour, and mix thoroughly. Melt butter in a small saucepan or *bain marie* (double boiler) on low heat. Add the melted butter to the egg mixture and beat until blended. Set aside for 15 minutes. Then, pour the mixture into Madeleine molds. (If possible, find the soft plastic type; they are the easiest ones to use.)

Bake in a preheated oven at 300°F. for about 10 minutes, or until golden. It is very important to not bake in a convection oven. Remove the molds from the oven. Cool the Madeleines on a baking rack, and sprinkle confectioner's sugar on top when still warm.

Chic Purple Delight Lunch

BEET SOUP WITH SOUR CREAM AND FINGERLING POTATOES (SOUPE DE BETTERAVES)

Serves 6

Two 1-pound cans sliced beets, with liquid reserved
3 small cucumbers, peeled and diced into small cubes
2 cups white vinegar
3½ cups sour cream
1 cup chopped dill
½ cup finely chopped scallions
1 cup cooked fingerling potatoes, whole
12 ice cubes

Place beets, with their juice, in a medium-size bowl. Thoroughly mix in the cucumbers, vinegar, and 3 cups of sour cream. Stir in ¾ cup dill and scallions. Chill for 2 to 4 hours.

Evenly divide soup among individual soup bowls. Garnish with remaining sour cream and dill, and the potatoes. Add two ice cubes to each bowl.

CLAFOUTIS WITH BLACK CHERRIES COMME À LA MAISON

Serves 6 to 8

¼ teaspoon unsalted butter
3 large eggs
⅔ cup granulated sugar
1 cup bleached flour
1 cup heavy cream (or milk)
1 teaspoon Cognac
1 teaspoon vanilla extract
1 pound canned pitted cherries, drained
1 tablespoon confectioners' sugar

Butter a 10-inch cake or pie pan. Set aside. Whisk eggs and sugar together, until light and frothy. Sprinkle flour on top. Whisk until smooth. Stir in heavy cream, Cognac, and vanilla extract.

Place cherries in the pan. Pour batter on top. Sprinkle with confectioners' sugar. Bake in preheated 350°F. oven until evenly puffed and brown, about 40 minutes. Remove pan from oven. Serve warm or at room temperature. You can substitute apples, pears, or clementines for the cherries.

Chic Cliché Lunch à la Française

CHIC QUICHE

Serves 6

¼ teaspoon unsalted butter

One 9-inch store-bought pie crust

3 eggs

1 cup milk (or heavy cream)

1 cup whipped cream cheese

½ pound Swiss cheese, grated

2 slices ham (smoked Black Forest is preferable),
cut into small pieces

¼ teaspoon fresh thyme leaves, coarsely chopped

Coarse sea salt, a pinch

Freshly ground black pepper, a pinch

Butter a 9-inch ceramic pie dish. Place the pie crust inside. In a small bowl, thoroughly mix eggs, milk, and cream cheese. Add Swiss cheese and ham. Sprinkle the thyme, salt, and pepper on top.

Bake in a preheated 350°F. oven until crust is brown, about 45 minutes. Remove dish from oven. Serve warm.

GRATED CARROTS WITH VINAIGRETTE CLASSIQUE

Serves 6

6 carrots, peeled

Vinaigrette Classique

½ bunch fresh flat-leaf parsley, finely chopped

Insert each carrot into the grater attachment of a Cuisinart or other food processor. When the carrots have been coarsely grated, transfer them into a medium-size serving bowl. Add the vinaigrette and mix well. Sprinkle parsley on top.

VINAIGRETTE CLASSIQUE

1 teaspoon Dijon mustard

1 teaspoon balsamic vinegar

4 teaspoons extra-virgin olive oil

Coarse sea salt, a pinch

Freshly ground black pepper, a pinch

Fresh thyme, a pinch

Optional:

1 large garlic clove, peeled

1 teaspoon freshly squeezed lemon juice

2 or 3 nasturtium flowers

Put mustard in a small bowl. Add vinegar and oil and mix well. Add salt, pepper, and thyme. Transfer to an empty jam jar. Cover and shake well. For stronger flavor, you can add a garlic clove or lemon juice. Decorate with nasturtium flowers from the garden.

Chic Tip: It is always good to make the vinaigrette in advance. Keep it stored in a jam jar in the pantry for a couple of months. You can also place a sprig of rosemary in the vinaigrette jar to infuse it with extra flavor. Never put the vinaigrette jar in the refrigerator.

Red Fruit Mousse with Raspberry Coulis and Fresh Mint

Serves 8

FOR THE MOUSSE:

1 cup fresh raspberries and strawberries, mixed

1 tablespoon granulated sugar

4 envelopes of Knox unflavored gelatin

2 eggs

1 cup heavy cream

FOR THE COULIS:

1 cup fresh raspberries

½ cup orange juice

1 dozen fresh mint leaves

To prepare the mousse:

Put the berries and sugar in a mixer, and blend well. Pour the fruit mixture into a saucepan and cook on low heat for 10 minutes. Add the gelatin and stir until dissolved. Pour the mixture into a medium-size bowl. Add the eggs, and mix thoroughly. Then stir in the heavy cream.

Fill eight small porcelain molds with the mixture. Cover each with foil and put them in the refrigerator. It is best to assemble the molds the night before.

To prepare the coulis:

In a bowl, blend together the raspberries, orange juice, and mint leaves. Put mixture in a saucepan and cook about 10 minutes on low heat. Let the mixture cool down.

To serve:

Remove the mousse from the molds and put on individual serving plates. Surround with berries and top each with about a tablespoon of raspberry coulis. Add a mint leaf as decoration.

ARUGULA SALAD WITH CHIVE FLOWERS AND VINAIGRETTE CLASSIQUE

Serves 4

1 pack arugula

1 dozen chive flowers (or nasturtium)

Vinaigrette Classique (see page 196 for recipe)

Wash arugula and dry it thoroughly on a cloth towel or in a salad spinner. You do not want a wet salad. Transfer to a serving bowl. Right before serving, pour the vinaigrette over the arugula, and toss to coat the leaves thoroughly. Make sure not to drown the arugula with too much vinaigrette. Garnish with chive flowers.

STUFFED RACK OF VEAL

Serves 6

1 pound spinach, washed and stemmed

½ pound fresh goat cheese

1 cup grated Parmigiano-Reggiano cheese

1 cup toasted pine nuts

½ cup roasted and peeled garlic cloves

2 large eggs

1 tablespoon minced fresh rosemary leaves

1 teaspoon coarse sea salt

½ teaspoon freshly ground white pepper

One 5½-pound rack of veal, bones trimmed of excess fat, butterflied with bones intact, and lightly pounded by a butcher

Coarse sea salt and freshly ground black pepper, to taste

2 tablespoons of extra-virgin olive oil

Place the spinach in a sauté pan. Cover and steam until wilted, about 30 seconds. Remove pan from heat. Place spinach in cold water. Drain. Wring dry in a towel. Set aside. Mix goat cheese, Parmigiano-Reggiano, pine nuts, roasted garlic, eggs, rosemary, salt, and white pepper together in a bowl. Set aside.

Unfold top piece of meat. The meat will lie almost flat. Season with salt and black pepper. Spread a thin layer of cheese mixture over meat. Cover with spinach. Spread the remaining cheese mixture on top. Roll meat back up to the bones. Tie a piece of twine in between each rib. Set aside.

Heat oil in a large sauté pan over high heat. Sear meat until brown, about 5 minutes. Remove pan from heat. Place rack in a roasting pan. Roast in a preheated 350°F.

oven until an internal thermometer reads 125°F., about 55 minutes. Remove rack from oven. Set aside for about 1/2 hour. Slice meat into individual chops. Serve at room temperature.

ZUCCHINI GRATIN

Serves 6 to 8

2 tablespoons extra-virgin olive oil

2 small cloves garlic, peeled

2 sprigs fresh thyme

6 medium zucchini, about 1 1/2 pounds, peeled and thinly sliced into rounds

5 large eggs

3 cups heavy cream

1 cup grated Swiss cheese

1 cup whipped cream cheese

Heat oil in a skillet over medium heat. Add garlic, 1 sprig thyme, and zucchini. Sauté, stirring frequently until zucchini is tender, about 8 minutes. Remove pan from heat. Discard garlic and thyme sprig. Set aside.

In a bowl, mix eggs, heavy cream, 3/4 cup of Swiss cheese, and whipped cream cheese, remaining thyme, and zucchini. Spread mixture evenly in a 10-inch gratin dish. Sprinkle remaining Swiss cheese on top.

Bake in a preheated 350°F. oven until top is brown and crisp, about 20 to 25 minutes. Remove pan from oven. Set aside for 15 minutes. Serve warm or at room temperature.

MY GRANDMOTHER'S CHOCOLATE CAKE (GÂTEAU AU CHOCOLAT DE MA GRANDMÈRE)

Serves 8 to 10

3/4 cup of water

3/4 cup granulated sugar

3/4 pound bittersweet chocolate

1/2 pound, plus 1 tablespoon, unsalted butter, cut into pieces

3 eggs

1 tablespoon all-purpose flour

1/4 cup cocoa powder

Place water and sugar in a saucepan over medium heat. Stir until sugar has dissolved. Boil for 1 minute. Reduce heat to low. Add chocolate. Stir until melted. Remove pan from heat. Add 1/2 pound butter. Stir until melted. Set aside to cool.

Lightly beat eggs, one at a time, in a large bowl. Stir in chocolate mixture. Whisk in flour.

Grease a 9-inch cake mold with remaining butter and pour in batter. Set cake mold in a large pan of hot water. The water should come halfway up the cake mold. Place the pan and cake mold on middle rack of a preheated 350°F. oven. Bake for 50 minutes. Do not bake in a convection oven.

Take the pan and cake mold out of the oven. Then remove the cake mold from the water bath, and cool on a baking rack overnight. Wrap the cake in foil and keep it in a cool place. Do not refrigerate. Before serving, sprinkle cocoa powder on top.

Chic Tips: It is best to make this cake the night before. Line the cake mold with foil. This will make your life easier when removing the cake from the mold. The foil will also protect your cake from breakage.

The Bedroom

In bed we laugh, in bed we cry
And, born in bed, in bed we die.
The near approach a bed may show
Of human bliss to human woe.
—Isaac de Benserade (1612–91)

FROM THE EARLIEST TIMES, great attention has been devoted to beds, and rightly so. We start our day in bed, and spend in it approximately eight hours. It is the first thing that we see and feel when we wake up. Many hours in our life (when you think of it, almost one-third of it!) are spent in bed. Sleep and rest are basic and vital human functions; without sleep, one certainly cannot function very well and may even perish.

Today, in an era in which we all seem to be burdened with too many activities, the bedroom is a heavenly cocoon, a sacred place where we can finally relax. And with all the activities related to sleeping (do I dare go into it?), it is also the most private part of our life. Oddly enough, it was not always the case. The notion of the bedroom as a haven is a fairly recent one. Right up to the nineteenth century, the bedroom was, believe it or not, a reception room.

The heavy curtains, a protection from the drafts, enveloped the bed. They were drawn open during the day, allowing daily interaction with a string of visitors. Particularly in the fifteenth and sixteenth centuries this room was used for bathing, meeting, and eating, sometimes all at once.

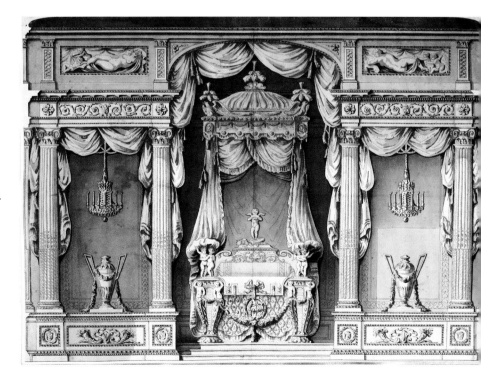

OPPOSITE: The master bedroom is a haven for reading and relaxing. The peaceful brown and ivory toile de Jouy color scheme is repeated throughout the room.

RIGHT: An eighteenth-century French ink drawing, c. 1770, of a state bedroom with a canopy bed. The Metropolitan Museum of Art, Purchase, Harris Brisbane Fund and Joseph Pulitzer Bequest, 1971.

A busy room! The reason is simple: Our ancestors were consistently spending more money on bed decoration and construction than on any other pieces of furniture. So they needed to show it off.

At that time, nobody thought of a bedroom as private sleeping quarters. The bed was shared with all members of the household and even guests were invited. Body heat is certainly the most economical form of heat! The impoverished, or *paysans*, even shared their bedroom with animals and such habits persisted until quite recently. I vividly remember twenty-five years ago visiting an old farmer in the French Alps. His cows were on the other side of his bedroom separated only by an open fence.

Beds, as we know now, were already in use in Egypt as early as 3000 B.C. (not exactly yesterday) with rectangular frames and straps to secure the mattress, supported on short legs sometimes carved in the form of animal feet. The animal motif was supposed to enhance the sleeper with great power. *Pourquoi pas?* Maybe a good cure for insomnia.

The following centuries and civilizations each put their own twist on the bed, but interestingly enough its basic shape has not changed much. The Greeks and Romans had variations on the same theme. The Middle Ages, however, saw some alterations. The less fortunate segment of the population slept on the floor while the landowner had his mattress placed upon a low wooden dais. The medieval bed was hung with bed curtains, which became more and more elaborate as the centuries passed. During the Renaissance, the superstructure became more complex in wealthier houses—a large canopy to protect the bed from dirt falling from the ceiling and side curtains to exclude both drafts and prying eyes. Voluminous pillows or bolsters (*polochon*) supporting the head and blankets became *un signe extérieur de richesse*—fur for the great lords, hemp for the hoi polloi.

For years the best blankets came from Chalon in France. The earliest mattresses were stuffed with feathers, straw, or wool—not quite the orthopedic comfort of today—and the bedbugs were no joke but a sad reality. Pillows, usually quite voluminous, supported the head and the upper body as the fashion dictated until the nineteenth century when it was chic to parade in the bedroom. In France, mattress, pillows, and bolsters were

usually composed of bags made of a kind of canvas called *coutil,* and were striped brown and white. Not everyone had sheets. Until the sixteenth century, only royals or the wealthy members of the aristocracy seemed to be able to afford them. Washing was done by hand! So imagine washing white linen in a cold river. Sheets, when you were wealthy enough to afford them, were mostly made of linen. They came in several qualities ranging from off-white to very white, in extreme cases enhanced with lace and gold thread, as were the sheets that Henri III of France used. However, Renaissance ladies such as Diane de Poitiers, a celebrated beauty and the mistress of King Henri II, preferred black satin sheets, for the contrast with her creamy white skin.

We have to wait until the end of the sixteenth century to see the bedroom achieve a decorative unity: wall hangings beginning to match the bed fabrics, and the chairs and carpets, in color and style. The type of bed that became by far the most popular in the seventeenth century was known all over Europe as a "French bed." *Bien sur!* The simple wooden framework of this type of bed supported the hangings to form a plain, rectangular box. There were no cornices running around the top; curtains hung straight down from the top rails. The simplest form of such beds had three curtains, one on each of the exposed sides that was nailed to the top rails. During daytime these curtains were tied up out of the way, with a cord. A more sophisticated version of this bed had curtains that could be moved horizontally on rods (like a window curtain). In this case, rods and rings were hidden by a valance. The status of the bed depended on the cost of the hangings, the magnificence of the trimmings, and the splendor of the *panaches,* often ostrich plumes.

During the seventeenth century, beds kept the same rectangular form, even for the grandest setting. They only grew taller and the richness of the trimmings continued to increase, as did the bedspread, which grew more elaborate as the years went by. The Sun King's bed was made to dazzle and astonish the visitor and inspire awe. A 1687 inventory of Louis XIV's bed at Versailles is described in minute detail: *Le lict est en forme de lict d'ange et admirablement beau, le pavillon est suspendu au toict avec des cordons et houppes d'or, qui les soustiennent par les petits enroullements dorés au coins du pavillon.* (The bed is in the form of an angel bed and is astonishingly beautiful. The tester is suspended from the ceiling by cords and tassels of gold which are held by little gilt scrolls at the corner of the tester.) It was the setting for an elaborate ritual known as the *levée,* which involved paying homage to the monarch, as he dressed, undressed, and got in and out of bed.

Royal bedrooms functioned as theaters. The bed was placed on a platform in an alcove, decorated with elaborate carving on the painted woodwork, and hung with materials hiding a service door. Behind the formal royal bedroom appeared the *petit appartement* where a more informal life coexisted with the more formal grandeur of the court life. The *petit appartement* combined splendor with comfort—*finalement.* It included a private bedroom where one could be alone with *intimes,* as well as a small elegant cabinet, known in the eighteenth century as a *boudoir.*

A tentlike canopy dresses up a young girl's bed and is a *clin d'oeil*—a wink— toward the tent-patterned wallpaper. The tent theme is picked up in the pelmets and curtains, keeping a whimsical spirit throughout the room.

The bold stripes of the wallpaper in this bedroom provide a tentlike feeling and are quite graphic and masculine. This decor is well suited to my son, who is a trophy-winning soccer player and a model-car collector.

La Marquise du Châtelet, among other accomplishments the patron, mistress, and intellectual companion of France's most famous philosopher and poet, Voltaire, had such a setting in her Château de Cirey. But while habits and heating systems may have changed, the structure of the bed has more or less remained the same, apart from head and footboards, which may be carved or upholstered (like today's fashion!).

In eighteenth-century France, as a general tendency toward nightly comfort emerged, fanciful names were invented for different types of canopies: *lit* à *colonnes*, supported on four visible wooden columns; à *la polonaise*, with curved iron supports forming a dome entirely swathed in fabric and curtains; à *la duchesse*, attached at the back of the wall or ceiling. Bed hangings were no longer simply functional, and fabric became more informal and came in an array of printed cottons, such as toile de Jouy, in bright colors to be better seen by candlelight.

The Empire saw a new bed shape, *en gondole,* on a slight platform with a small footstool to climb aboard. The material would be draped only on one side with a *ciel* from which the curtain could drop and envelop the bed. It had an air of elegant simplicity, which was genuinely new. Then, around 1820, the height of the bed dropped, a result of the invention of the box spring.

Bedrooms exert tremendous evocative power on our lives; their effect is long-lasting and pervasive. Marcel Proust, too, had powerful memories of the bedrooms in which he had lived: *I envisioned now one, now another of the bedrooms I had occupied in my life, and eventually I remembered all of them in long daydreams that filled the time after I woke up.* Today, for most of us, bedrooms are our sanctuary, our hidden heaven, even if in recent years some are becoming multitasking spaces with the addition of an entertainment center, exercise machine, dressing room, and laptop computer. Modernity moves on. Where is the *boudoir* when you need it? *Dormez bien.*

Chic Advice

- If you are buying an antique bed, remember that king-size did not exist before the twentieth century.

- If clean lines and practicality matter to you, a metal frame is the way to go.

- Comfortable duvets are pretty and easy to use. Their covers can be washed and ironed in a flash.

- Mattress pads in down or wool will make your bed extra-delicious. Do not skimp on the quality of your mattress.

- I like pale colors on bedroom walls. I am partial to old-fashioned toile. It is peaceful and subtle. An upholstered headboard is a must in my view, comfortable, simple, and not overly expensive. Remember high and low. Simplicity is good in my view, more conducive to light dreams.

- You have been dreaming of a romance in an all-white bedroom with comfy pillows, the softest cotton or linen. Satin and dark colors do not do it for me. Surprisingly enough, flannel sheets in the winter are delightfully comfy, especially after being washed again and again. Try it! Design and cleanliness go hand in hand for a luxurious and restful bedroom. Sweet dreams. Do not let the bedbugs bite.

TOILE DE JOUY: SIMPLE PLEASURES

Once again, history repeats itself. Once upon a time a king, a queen, and their courtiers sported novel fabrics for their waistcoats and dresses in their palaces. By the 1780s, fashion (we all know how finicky fashion can be) favored little vignettes of allegorical scenes, contemporary events, or romanticized rustic courtships in the style of the painters Watteau and Fragonard. These scenes were printed in single colors, either red in a manner of a red chalk drawing, or blue in imitation of the chinoiserie patterns on blue-and-white china. This type of printed cotton was immensely popular by the late eighteenth century, for both furnishings and clothing. Louis XVI and his queen, Marie Antoinette, loved it and so did the following rulers—the latter without losing their heads! The fabric became universally known as toile de Jouy after its town of origin.

Today's new hot fashion for summer clothing, as well as for home upholstery, is the same cotton print, the toile. It is at your fingertips everywhere: blue-and-white toile design sheets at Target, blue or red toile duvet covers and shams in the Pottery Barn catalogue, yellow toile pillows at Pierre Deux, fancy skirts or pants in green toile at Scoop in New York City, without even mentioning the myriad of fancy fabric houses in design centers throughout the country who carry variations in a multitude of color combinations. The choice is all yours.

It all began in India. The Indus Valley was one of the birthplaces of cotton (the other was Peru). Textile remnants found at the site of Mohenjo-Daro prove that cotton was produced there as early as the second millennium B.C. Cotton slowly but surely traveled the world. From India its cultivation spread to the Persian Gulf, then to Egypt and the Mediterranean. Islamic traders introduced it to Africa. The Chinese farmed cotton and were followed by the Koreans, whose methods were adopted by the Japanese during the sixteenth century.

Although North American Indians began growing cotton, sometime between A.D. 700 and 1000, much of the New World economy rested on the plantation system developed during the colonial period, and ultimately on the slave trade. Vessels loaded with European trinkets sailed from Nantes or Bristol for African ports, where they exchanged their merchandise for human cargo, which in turn was traded for cotton, tobacco, and sugar in America, to be then sold on the Continent.

European countries kept the importation of cotton in check by legislation, partly to protect their local production of silks and wools. The Marquise de Pompadour, the sophisticated and powerful mistress of the French King Louis XV, and the unofficial fashion ruler of the time, is credited with the lifting of the French ban in 1759. Cotton was finally allowed! Soon, various ways to embellish it were created, copperplate printing being one. Copperplate printing achieved its greatest triumphs primarily at the factory that Christophe-Philippe Oberkampf founded in 1760 at Jouy-en-Josas, a village on the outskirts of Paris. Oberkampf developed colorfast dyes and a method of printing using engraved metal roller presses that gave precise definition to his designs, setting them apart from fabrics printed with crude wood blocks. The cotton toiles produced at Jouy gave their name to a textile genre whose popularity continues unabated to this day. His success was due to various factors: the proximity

Variations of toile can work together. Even though the headboard fabric and wallpaper have different patterns, they complement each other. The large white piping separating each toile downplays their differences.

of the factory to Versailles, so that the courtiers made a practice of visiting it, a keen eye for changes in taste, and a readiness to adapt new techniques and the industrial method of production. Oberkampf survived the Revolution and by 1797 he was able to turn out 5,000 yards of printed cloth a day! Not bad for a pre-industrialization production.

One of the attractions of toile, in addition to its pleasing monochrome visual effect, was its picture book quality, documenting the achievements, pleasures, and preoccupations of the era. Finally, this printed cotton existed without saccharine flower motifs in a multiplicity of shades. The attraction of toile was its simple color scheme, usually a single color such as blue, red, green, or black on a white background, which gave it a bold look. In addition to the well-known four seasons, elements, and corners of the world, the holy sacraments, and famous monuments, the cottons were decorated with images of fashionable chinoiserie, recently discovered Pompeii paintings, and subjects from literature (including La Fontaine's fables), mythology, and history. Current events provided the most edifying examples—"nobles savages" abounded, and young America was shown rendering

grateful homage to France. The success of this fabric, of course, created competition, and by the end of the nineteenth century France boasted three hundred toile manufacturers. Today numerous companies have followed in their footsteps very successfully, having added many more color schemes.

Toile de Jouy looks its best in the home when used in abundance, specifically for curtains, pillows, bedcovers, sheets, and on the walls. The opposite is true for clothing. For a dress or skirt, less is more. Avoid head to toe! Contrast in patterns and texture adds interest, especially in bedrooms where I think toile works best as it creates a cozy, yet restful, environment. It is an easy way to create a sophisticated look for the bedroom at minimal expense, as there are so many available sources.

Nowadays some companies, such as Pierre Deux, are even offering wallpaper with designs to match their toile fabric as a cheaper alternative to the old-fashioned way of upholstering the walls. The effect is lovely, and the wallpaper easy to apply. Try it. Also, keep in mind that one of the many advantages of cotton toile is that it can be washed.

OPPOSITE, CLOCKWISE FROM TOP LEFT: Toile de Jouy often commemorated current events. This example on linen uses Neoclassical motifs and themes to celebrate the new American republic.

This toile is a classic blue-and-white on cotton. The urns and flowers give it a Neoclassical feel.

Even the armchair is upholstered in the toile motif; this fabric is similar to the one used for the curtain.

Detail of a toile de Jouy composed of vignettes depicting the pleasures of the farm printed on a white ground.

The Bathroom

Je me suis baigné dans le Poème

De la Mer . . .

Devorant les azurs verts

(I bathe myself

In the poetic Ocean

Devouring the green azures)

—Arthur Rimbaud (1854–91)

FUNNILY ENOUGH, bathrooms have existed as far back as antiquity. But they were not always what they are today—a private place. Around the second or third century most large cities of the Roman Empire were equipped with public baths. Baths played an important part in everyday life as the ancients realized the power of cleanliness! Public baths were used not only for cleanliness and related activities, such as massage, cool pool, hot-slipper bath, and steam—*mais oui*—but also for physical activities, as a gym really, and for intellectual exchanges. It became the perfect spot to share the day's gossip. As a matter of fact, the public bath was the center of one's social life. It was definitely healthier than a bar! Its large size made it possible to accommodate a number of people in rooms devoted to a variety of purposes. In cooler climates, the public bath was probably the only warm place. It was very enticing indeed, at a time when people had no source of heat at home other than braziers. In cold weather, they wore overcoats inside as well as on the streets.

As the centuries went by, slight changes in customs transpired. First, friends gathered at private homes and then went to the baths, but not to one of the large ones, instead to a smaller establishment designed to respect personal

OPPOSITE: Wallpaper is always a good way to warm up a bathroom. An old-fashioned mirror from Pottery Barn and sconces give an old-world touch to this otherwise modern bathroom in the pool house. A classic washstand from Waterworks stands on a chic marble floor. I love to mix high and low!

RIGHT: The luxurious shower, a Waterworks Easton combination, is enhanced with unusual *verde imperial* marble. It gives a sleek sheen to the pool house.

Mirror mirror on the wall, I'm my ...
after all

...een drinking
... to stay until
... remember—
... mean it

modesty. The Romans slowly started to develop a new attitude toward the body. This also reflected the aristocratic desire to stand apart from the crowd, making the wealthy more independent of communal life. In turn, this development went hand in hand with the increasing formalization of the social hierarchy. This stands in contrast to today's behavior of everybody mingling half-naked at the gym. This aristocratic desire explains the proliferation of private baths in private houses. Private baths were frequently added to existing dwellings or enlarged from smaller facilities. Eventually they became commonplace.

Roman bathrooms were quite sophisticated, decorated with mosaics on the walls and floors, painted murals, and boasted such refined amenities as radiant heat. *Et oui déjà!* The walls and floors were heated with hot-water pipes. We have not invented anything too far removed from this. Unfortunately the subsequent civilizations and centuries were not as sophisticated. The Middle Ages saw bathing as a shared experience. Communal bathing then was more a matter of convenience than a useful experience of lascivious intent. Members of the opposite sex, guests, and family bathed together simply because heating a fresh supply of water for every individual in the household would have been impractical.

The notion of people entertaining in their bathroom is somewhat linked to this custom. It was considered a rare honor to be granted an audience while the king was at his *toilette*. This is a totally different twist on the way the ancients were thinking. When invited to share an aristocrat or a king's intimate gestures, you were made to feel that you were close to him.

Chic Advice

- If you have an old bathtub, reglazing is an inexpensive option.
- White for a bathtub or sink is the best color. For the bathroom walls, white accented with another color is always a good choice.
- Always try to separate the toilet and bathtub. This will make the space more luxurious.
- Make sure that there is adequate lighting close to the mirror.

OPPOSITE: Antique fixtures and mirrors are welcome choices for a bathroom or powder room.

ABOVE: Miniature paintings as well as decorative details add charm to a bathroom.

The Peripatetic Life of a Bathtub

Early versions of the sixteenth-century bathtub were made of wood, sometimes copper, often with a linen hood and lining to keep out drafts, reduce the cold touch of marble or metal, or the clammy feel of a wooden *baignoire*. Those bathtubs were always placed in the bedchamber (a little room off the bedroom) in front of a large fire, the only source of heat then. We are far away from the radiant heat of our Roman ancestors!

As time went on and means increased, bathtubs became more sophisticated, and sometimes were even disguised as a piece of furniture. One memorable bathtub belonged to Marie Leszczynska, Louis XIV's wife, Queen of France. It was made of copper with Dutch tiles on the walls of the tub and the room. This high-sided bathtub with neck-high water became the rage; some can still be found today. Another splendid bathtub was located in the *appartement des bains* at Versailles that had been fitted for Madame de Montespan, Louis XIV's mistress. It was a luxurious flat consisting of a suite of rooms that included an antechamber, *une chambre de repos,* a room with a day-bed, *une pièce des cuves* with two bathtubs, one for washing and one for rinsing, and *un cabinet de chaises* (or loo) for good measure. Incidentally, a common French name for close-stool, or toilette, was *lieu d'aisance*, which was shortened to *lieu* (hence in English, loo.) The walls were completely faced with several types of marble with a painted and gilded ceiling. The bathtub was hewn from a single piece of marble, brought from Brittany. Fashioned in the shape of a modern hot tub, it had steps to descend into the water, a bench around the inside, and pipes made of leather. Louis XIV spent many enjoyable hours in that private *appartement,* according to his biographers. You can hardly blame him; this was the fringe benefit of kingly duty.

If one did not have the facilities at home for taking a bath, one could hire a bathtub for a moderate sum or go to a public bathhouse. A popular book on etiquette, *La Loi de la Galanterie Française,* published in 1640, recommended *l'on peut aller quelque fois chez les baigneurs pour avoir le corps net.* (One can occasionally go to the bathhouse to keep the body clean.) The book also advised the gentry that daily ablutions are a good idea: *Tous les jours l'on prendra la peine de se laver avec le pain d'amande. Il faut aussi se laver le visage aussi souvent.* (Every day one should take the trouble to wash with *pain d'amande*. It is also important to wash one's face almost as often.) At the time, this was a novel idea for most of the population.

Both Voltaire and his mistress and benefactor, the Marquise du Châtelet, believed in bathing, which was a bit against the general custom of the time despite the recommendation of *La Loi de la Galanterie Française.* Many of their learned contemporaries thought that bathwater made the body porous and thus open to miasma, which could enter the skin. At Cirey, her country château, the couple created an entirely separate *appartement des bains,* with its own antechamber, chamber, and *cabinet de toilette,* modeled after Louis XIV's.

The nineteenth century saw a return to privacy; bathrooms were not meant to be shared anymore, except possibly with your lover. The Napoleonic era gave birth to even more elaborate bathrooms lavishly enhanced with marble, paintings, mosaics, and statues. Bathtubs were frequently made of bronze or cast iron, with faucets of solid gold. Bathtubs moved from being in the middle of the room to against a wall, but fireplaces were still the only source of heat.

Napoleon I had a sophisticated *salle de bain* at the Château de Rambouillet, with a copper bathtub surrounded by painted and gilded walls with, *bien sûr,* Empire motifs—swans, griffins, and deity figures bearing laurel branches.

Today bathtubs can be placed wherever your heart desires—in the middle of the room, against the wall, or even in front of a window. A fireplace can be installed for a decorative effect; it is a wonderful luxurious addition. Increasingly, even in contemporary houses, people seem to be turning their bathroom, particularly the master bathroom a haven, a place to relax and unwind. In order to do so, they often choose big bathtubs with chunky claw feet, giving the

LEFT: We kept the original cast-iron bathtub in this guest bathroom. The tub is so large, heavy, and beautiful that it would have been a shame to get rid of it. Instead we had it reglazed and installed new fixtures. The tub is now like new, but only better.

RIGHT: The Waterworks bathtub is a new addition to this bathroom, one that is totally in keeping with the spirit of the house. The beadboard is white and the walls above it are pale aqua. In the guest bathroom, pictured at left, we reversed the color treatment.

salle de bain a look of yesterday alongside modern comforts. People are craving glamour and the bathroom is certainly the place to start trying to reach the level of luxury of the past. For example, a tub carved from a single piece of marble is not a bad idea at all. *Vive la baignoire!*

The Orangerie, Jardin d'hiver, & Greenhouse

Ils pressent les oranges et jetent la peau.

(They squeeze the orange and throw away the skin.)

—Voltaire (1694–1778), letter to Madame Denis, September 2, 1751

(referring to his quarrel with Frederick the Great)

CHARLES VIII OF FRANCE erected the first large greenhouse intended specifically for oranges—an *orangerie* at his Château d'Amboise around 1493. Soon the fashion spread. The châteaux of the royals and nobility were not complete without their own increasingly splendid *orangeries*. The magnificent *orangerie* at Versailles, designed by Jules Hardouin Mansart for Louis XIV, was the culmination. It took two years to build from its inception in 1684. Its plan and construction were completed before the château itself. The king, a fanatical gardener, had a special interest in orange trees. He adored their subtle and distinct perfume and

OPPOSITE: The peaceful *jardin d'hiver* (garden room) is decorated with a mix of personal objects—from the white tree-trunk table to the lavender taffeta curtains with leaf appliqué and the white duck cotton-covered sofa. Plants look good at different heights; this room, with its high ceilings, allows for that.

RIGHT: A cast-iron nineteenth-century planter placed on a pedestal holds exuberant ferns year-round.

attributed to that special tree aphrodisiac powers of sorts. The *orangerie* is still in existence today. Located in the *Parterre du Midi* at Versailles, benefiting from a southern exposure, it is shaped like a square with one side missing, and is more than 1,000 feet in circumference. *Très grande*. Over a thousand orange and lemon trees, planted in distinctive *caissons* (square planters), were stored in the *orangerie* in the winter, then wheeled outside during the milder months, from May to October, lined up like soldiers at the ready—the *Parterre Bas*. Following the royal orders, the king's gardeners would keep a number of the trees in bloom year-round, replacing them at fifteen-day intervals. Specimens were brought from all over Italy and even Santo Domingo.

OPPOSITE: In the corner of the *jardin d'hiver* is an old stone sink, perfect for watering plants. It is also used as a bar. Versatility is a plus in interior decoration.

ABOVE: The mix of high and low continues in this pale lavender room with its collection of unusual objects, including the three-tier marble *présentoire* and a coffee table made to look like a massive tree trunk—a slice has been taken out for a final whimsical twist. A marble bust adds a touch of romance.

This was an expansive hobby. The Duchesse de La Ferté paid 2,200 livres (about $10,000 today) for twenty orange trees. Like favorite pets, the trees had names. It is recorded that one known as *Le Grand Bourbon* was planted in 1491 by the Princesse de Navarre, moved by François I to Fontainebleau, and then moved again by Louis XIV to Versailles. In 1966, Nancy Mitford wrote that eight specimens of the original orange trees that belonged to the Sun King were still alive in the garden at Versailles after more than three hundred years.

Louis XIV used his *orangerie* as an indoor pleasure garden, a place of awe and inspiration for foreign dignitaries, as well as the site of brilliant receptions and balls, for which he decorated it with exotic palm trees and a myriad of rare flowers. As many as two million pots of flowers were brought out of the greenhouse in the winter and kept in the garden for short periods of time to appear as if flowers grew outside all year. Needless to say, *orangeries* sprung up in short order throughout Europe, from Brussels to Postdam and Schöenbrunn.

Orangeries were usually stone constructions, built in an estate's garden and featuring a southern exposure and a ceiling height calculated for maximum thermal protection. They housed a vast range of exotic plants all winter long, and are the ancestors of the greenhouse. Even the conservative George Washington joined in the fun, and in 1780 built a heated glass conservatory at Mount Vernon.

The *jardin d'hiver* was the child of the *orangerie*. These *jardins* began to appear in the first half of the nineteenth century and proliferated rapidly during the Second Empire as a result of the enormous infatuation with exotic flowers and rare plants fueled by universal exhibitions. In the nineteenth century, a *jardin d'hiver*, or greenhouse, was the real mark of a home of distinction and was attached to the side of the house off the *salon*—the classic arrangement. The most widely imitated model was the winter garden of a *hôtel particulier* on the rue de Courcelles in Paris belonging to Princess Mathilde, the granddaughter of Napoleon I and the subject of numerous renderings or paintings. Princess Mathilde received many artists and writers in this *hôtel*, which was given to her in 1857 by her cousin, Napoleon III. Illuminated from above through a glass roof, the *jardin d'hiver* was filled with plants, bushes, ivy, and palms, which brought nature right into the heart of Paris.

At the time, writers used winter gardens to set the stage. Emile Zola, for example, made sure that the rich speculator Saccard was equipped with one, a perfect *signe extérieur de richesse*. In the era of Proust's *salon*, the winter garden added a note of distinction to a home. Only the well-heeled could afford to have a drink and sit beneath palm trees while snow or sleet fell outside. These sophisticated indoor gardens always faced inward, opening into a courtyard or a private garden—a special secret oasis of ultimate luxury, representing man's domination over nature through money.

To this day, both structures, either a greenhouse away from the main house, or a conservatory attached to the house, is a luxury and a rare pleasure. However, modern life makes it

The *jardin d'hiver* is a multi-purpose space. The room's light is beautiful during the day, making it a wonderful alternative spot for lunch or tea. The table is set for a cozy winter lunch.

possible to buy ready-made greenhouse kits or even conservatories, making such structure much more affordable and practical. *Vive le progrès.*

Plants give life to a home, especially in the winter when it is more difficult to have cut flowers. Rare is the house without some flowering plant in it. Orange and lemon trees can be readily found and cared for quite easily now: Their sweet perfume can be enjoyed by all. Oranges are no longer a costly rarity, but an everyday commodity that can be picked up at the supermarket. Plants reveal as much about the nature of a homeowner as the owner's dog! People who enjoy plants usually have a better insight on life and seem to be more understanding than those who have no use for them. Flowers are the living food of the spirit—a symbol of life itself. *Les fleurs et les plantes représentent la vie.*

Chic Advice

- Plants are divided in two groups: flowering and foliage (leafy) types.

- Light is the most important factor in governing the growth of plants. Sunlight is needed to produce buds on nearly every flowering plant. Foliage plants typically survive well without direct sunlight.

- Another important factor is temperature. Plants are like people. Some like it hot, some like it cool. The best temperature for most plants in the winter is 70 degrees F. during the day and 55 degrees F. at night, with a few exceptions such as African violets.

- One reason our grandmothers grew better houseplants than we do now is because room temperatures were lower then, especially at night. You were dying of pneumonia but your plants survived beautifully.

- Watering is also important for the good health of your plants, and it is an art. A good way to water is to set the plant, pot and all, half submerged in the sink. After the plant is completely saturated, allow the surplus water to drain off.

- You can graduate to your own greenhouse and do like Louis XIV, rotating your flowering marvels every fifteen days in and out of your castle.

For me, the greenhouse is a source of infinite delight. Tired plants get rejuvenated after a short stay and new ones become strong before being planted in the garden outside.

The Garden

On doit cultiver notre jardin. (We must cultivate our garden.)

—Voltaire (1694–1778), *Candide*, 1759

THE GARDEN inspires artists, poets, philosophers, and painters. It elevates the mind and the soul. Nothing is more satisfying than nature domesticated, tamed, and improved by art as displayed in the classical French gardens. Remember Villandry, with those exquisitely traced *parterres* of vegetables.

On Louis XIV's orders, the garden designer André Le Nôtre (1613–1700) transformed Versailles from a swampy wilderness into an oasis of symmetrical beauty, framed by rare specimen trees, classical *fontaines* and statues, and with precisely drawn canals dominated by a central axis. The king loved his gardens so much that he not only spent a vast fortune on them, he almost died among his beloved orange trees and topiaries.

The art of landscape gardening is to turn *le désordre* of nature into order and harmony. The "bones" of a garden are often mentioned when describing the underpinnings and structural outlines that form the foundation for its flowers, shrubs, trees, topiaries, grottoes, and gazebo. These are architectural features that

enhance the beds, *bosquets,* and *parterres,* and *met en valeur*—enhance—their best features. Such a skeleton is essential for any garden. This is why I favor structured gardens. Throughout the seasons these gardens always look good, even with snow on the ground. Once you have established their basic structure, they are quite forgiving. *Mais oui.* French opera would turn the garden into a magical place

OPPOSITE: My beloved topiary trees, combined with a wisteria arbor, add drama and mystery to the garden. The structure of the trees is striking, even during the winter months when the garden is under the snow.

RIGHT: Indoors and outdoors should always be treated as part of the total concept. In the garden, as in the house, I love contrasts. Here, the luxuriousness of rugosa roses is seen against a simple clean white picket fence—abundance next to structure.

TOP: A quiet moment in the garden.

ABOVE: A family game of croquet on the lawn.

OPPOSITE, CLOCKWISE FROM TOP LEFT: This perspective from the balcony provides a direct view of the pool, which is quite far away. The faux tree table and chairs are nineteenth-century French.

Centennial maple trees shade the front lawn.

Topiaries punctuate the grounds. Some have been artfully placed close to the house.

The gardens, kept in check by their boxwood border, are in bloom. Once again, the French influence!

OVERLEAF: The recently completed pool house is a classically inspired structure that I designed and constructed to replace a dilapidated building. The addition of a medallion to the center of the pediment and metal urns on the roofline creates balance.

capable of melting even the coldest of hearts. Who would not become a romantic surrounded by fragrant, blooming tuberoses? In the paintings of Watteau, Boucher, and Fragonard, the garden is an enchanting place imbued with almost magical power, reflecting beauty and charm on the sitter.

Gardens are really the continuation of the house—its introduction, its frame, and its finishing touch. We are all well aware that a charming landscape increases immensely the value of a property. Beautiful gardens start with planning, structure, and organization. Repetition of a theme, along with punctuation points created by shrubs, *bosquets*, boxwood hedges, or topiaries, create structure in the garden. I love topiaries for their playfulness, as well as their structure. (This is sort of contradictory, but true!) Topiary is the art of embellishing a garden with plants that have been given specific shapes through cutting and clipping. Boxwood, yew, linden, and fruit trees are commonly used. Shapes can vary from the geometric—rectangular, conical, triangular, round, and spiral—to the playful with animals of various kinds and forms. As a sign of how large the garden business is today, topiaries are available in many pre-made shapes at numerous garden centers, and even at Home Depot. The art of topiary is becoming very democratic indeed. Who would have thought that Louis XIV's carefully designed topiaries for Versailles would end up at commercial garden centers!

Like so many other things in fashion today, topiaries are rooted in ancient as well as in French history. Topiary began as ancient art that was already appreciated in 700 B.C. in Assyria. The world "topiary" is derived from the ancient Greek word, *topos,* which means place. This art was developed by the Greeks, and later the Romans who explored with great creativity the malleability of certain species such as boxwood, laurel, cypress, and myrtle. Their capable gardeners imitated the great marble sculptures of the time to create works of art using plants. Topiary

became one more way of domesticating nature. The *Toscane* country villa of the writer Pliny the Younger reputedly had its grounds embellished with a multiplicity of boxwood and cypress shaped like wild animals and mythological figures, dispersed among priceless statues. Like other wealthy Romans' gardeners, Pliny's were Egyptian and Persian slaves who re-created scenes of their lost countries. Through them Romans learned how to appreciate this special natural art. The antique glory of the art of topiaries resurfaced in full force in sixteenth-century Italy. From there, topiary made its way to France in the following century, amplifying and beautifying ornamental gardens, deliniating decorative vegetable gardens, and framing palisades, green arbors, and espalier fruit trees (a method in which fruit trees are trained to grow flat—another favorite of mine). The great landscape architect Le Nôtre first worked his *magie* at Vaux-le-Vicomte, then at Versailles, where his gardens became the ultimate standard of taste as well as a major setting for court life. Topiary specimens lined elaborate parterres, framing vistas and lavish water displays, on a breathtaking scale.

Topiary is a total architectural wonder made of living greenery, shaped and pruned by the human hand that created it. Such an art form was an integral part of most European palaces, a necessary extension of all grand houses. Today, after years of neglect, topiaries are back in fashion. Just be aware of not overdoing them, and keep them in proportion with the rest of your plants. The fun part is that numerous varieties of plants can become a living work of art with a good cut. However, the ones with a slow growth—boxwood, yew, or ivy—are the best because they will keep their shape the longest and are able to resist the cold (essential in the Northeast, my part of the world). For complicated forms, such as animals, a wire carcass is usually necessary. After two or three years, you just have to follow the shape while pruning to maintain it. Pruning keeps the topiary outlines looking crisp.

Chic Advice

- The best plants for topiaries are boxwood, honeysuckle, holly, ivy, yew, laurel, privet, arbor vitae, cypress, and myrtle.

- When cutting, do not rely on the naked eye. Always have a ruler, a leveler, and a cord. And always place a cord in the same manner to maintain consistency in your pruning. Remember to stand back regularly while pruning. It is hard to get perspective on what you are doing if you stand too close. Follow as much as possible the existing shape of a plant. Never cut any of the interior branches. Trim only a little bit at a time, and take your time when pruning. Keep your tools sharp.

- Fall is a great time to do a bit of a trimming on your topiaries.

THE KITCHEN GARDEN: LA MAGIE DES HERBES

Trois et quatre fois heureux celui qui plante des choux.
(Oh trice and four times happy those who plant cabbages!)
— François Rabelais (1494–1553)

Some of the most famous French kitchen gardens, including those at Versailles, Vaux-le-Vicomte, and Chantilly, were designed and created by Jean-Baptiste de La Quintinie (1626–88). This brilliant *jardinier* perfected the techniques of pruning and transplanting, and created among other things the *espalier* method. The Sun King's vegetable garden, created between 1678 and 1683, benefited from a remarkable irrigation and drainage system, in addition to cold frames and greenhouses. It is an exceptional orchard-herbs-vegetable garden, the shape of which has hardly changed in three centuries. *Pas mal!* This garden was famous for supplying the royal table with asparagus in December, cauliflowers in March, strawberries in April, and melons in June. Pineapples and coffee beans were grown as well. *Imagine!* In the warm months fig trees grew in pots outside the gardener's lodgings, and the extensive orchard offered as many as fifty varieties of pears and apples. Fragrant herbs, fines herbes, and bouquet garni seasoned the elaborate feast. Of course, few of us can boast about such a kitchen garden. However, it is good to dream and we can always try. Fresh fruit and vegetables are nature's bounty and herbs enhance our lives. I love their fragrant aroma and their fresh, strong flavor that improves home cooking in an instant.

If you have the good fortune to have space for a kitchen garden, go ahead and plant one. It does not need to be nine acres like Versailles's *potager*. It could be as little as a few small beds or pots near your kitchen door. You will have the pleasurable task of organizing and designing it. Creating a kitchen garden is the ultimate artistic venture since you need to deal with three-dimensional shapes and forms that have texture and color, as well as the evocative powers of scent. If your space is relatively limited, despite the advice of our eminent philosophers, do not grow cabbages. Instead, you can grow a few versatile herbs with a heavenly scent.

Early civilizations had medical and mystical treatises about the sacred properties of several hundred plants. There were numerous herbs used for flavoring food, beauty treatments, crafts, and even celebrations. The recognition of a large number of herbs continued through Greek and Roman societies to Europe. Charlemagne, the king of the Franks and later the emperor of the West, was a highly organized man and

OPPOSITE: The hammock with its gentle movement in the shade is a welcoming spot for the hardworking.

ABOVE Nasturtiums are ready for picking. Fragrant herbs and vegetables, protected against invaders by attractive fencing, grow peacefully for our pleasure.

an energetic builder. In 812 A.D. he ordered a list of herbs to be grown on all imperial farms. In a poetic moment, this great warrior supposedly gave this definition of herbs: *Herbs were the friend of physicians and the glory of cooks.* So follow in his august footsteps and grow a nice selection of these friends.

Now it's time to make your garden. First, choose a site that has at least three-quarters of the area in a sunny location. Most herbs, like vegetables, prefer a slightly alkaline soil, and most need good drainage. Fortunately, herbs are among the easiest to grow of all plants. Insects don't bother them; apparently the fragrances that are so delightful to us smell terrible to bugs. Herbs are virtually immune to plant diseases as well. Any space will do, provided that it has partial sun. If the site is open, consider a break—either with a low stone wall, a fence, or hedge of low shrubs for privacy—to confine the perfumes for your own pleasure and give a settled atmosphere where bees and butterflies can work undisturbed. A fence is a good idea to protect your precious herbs from predators of all sizes. A slightly larger kitchen garden needs a path. It is important to plan the path well. Its design and material will create the style of your garden.

Herbs are such exuberant plants that they need some form of discipline or frame as a contrast. A geometric path offers just that. It provides bones for a garden during the dreary winter months, and, of course, on a practical note provides access to the plants. An edge made of boxwood is a very French way to go about this.

Select the material for your path with care. Grass and gravel can look attractive but require some upkeep. Which do you prefer? Mowing and raking are both good for your arm muscles, so the choice is yours.

Of course, hard surfaces last longest and materials such as old bricks and stone slabs offer the most beautiful colors. They are sometimes hard to find and can be an expensive proposition.

Herbs enrich our lives as they serve and delight us. Their fresh scents will flavor food like nothing else and instantly make your cooking reach the stratosphere. The beauty of herbs is that they enhance the natural flavor of a food, rather than mask it.

If this is going to be your first herb garden, there is great advantage in limiting yourself to only six or eight plants for ease and simplicity and for mastering the growth and cultivation of herbs. This way your investment in time and trouble is cut to a minimum. But if planting even eight varieties scares you, don't hesitate to grow fewer. If I could only plant one herb, I most certainly would choose basil. Its flavor is necessary for so many fresh summer dishes.

Keep in mind that some herbs are perennials, coming back year after year—some, like mint, are as invasive as weeds—whereas basil plants are annuals, which require replanting every year. When growing only six or eight plants, the most practical shape is the rectangle. It is also dignified by a long tradition. Medieval herb gardens, old French farmhouse gardens, and early colonists' gardens all had a rectangular shape. It is the simplest and easiest to work with. A simple method is to separate your rectangle in two. Then create four small sub-rectangles in each section. The result is a grid containing all the various herbs. For a most pleasing effect, make the lines straight. Now the big question: Which herbs should we select? For me, the basic herbs that fulfill all of my cooking requirements are basil, thyme, chives, parsley, rosemary, dill, mint, and lavender.

Basil (*basilic*). Sweet basil (rhymes with "dazzle") is an annual and grows 18 to 24 inches high. The flowers are small, white, and spiked. You don't want them to come to full bloom as that weakens the plant and dries up the aromatic oils. You can grow them from seed. Germination only takes about six days. Basil is slightly diuretic; it facilitates the digestion.

Chives (*ciboulette*). A member of the onion family, chives are perennials that grow 8 to 10 inches high. It's best to start them from plants. They are very hardy and grow well indoors.

Dill (*aneth*). This annual grows to a height of about 3 feet and is easily grown from seed. Germination takes ten to twelve days.

Lavender (*lavande*). This herb is a hardy perennial. The main secret to growing it is to use a large quantity of pulverized limestone. One of the most resistant and fragrant varieties of lavender is the Grosso, also called Lavandin.

Mint (*menthe*). There are many varieties of mint, all of which are hardy perennials. Start with one plant; if you're not careful, its offspring will spread so rapidly as to be a nuisance.

Parsley (*persil*). This hardy biannual is usually grown as an annual because the leaves are crisper the first year. Parsley is often considered hard to grow, probably because of its remarkably long germination period, which is three to six weeks. To mark the row, it is wise to mix a few radish seeds in. Partial shade is safer than full sun. Parsley is excellent for your complexion.

Rosemary (*romarin*). A tender perennial, rosemary looks like a miniature pine tree. In the Northeast, the winter is too cold so this plant needs to be moved indoors. It is easy to propagate with layering or cuttings. Use 6-inch pieces of new growth and let them stand with two-thirds of their length in wet sand until they take root. Rosemary is known to help fight off colds and the flu.

Thyme (*thym*). Many species exist but the best variety for a kitchen garden is the English, broad leaf version of *Thymus vulgaris*. It is a perennial and grows to a height of about 12 inches. Sometimes in the Northeast, if the winter is really cold, it dies. You can grow it from seed, and germination takes about ten days. Thyme is also good for the digestion and blood circulation.

A small picturesque French bistro-inspired chair surrounded by exotic potted plants near the pool awaits its sitter.

Chic Resources

Furnishings, Accessories, Tabletop, and Garden

A La Vieille Russie
781 Fifth Avenue
New York, New York 10022
(212) 752-1727

Anthropologie
(800) 309-2500
www.anthropologie.com

Baccarat
625 Madison Avenue
New York, New York 10022
(212) 826-4100
www.baccarat.com

Chinese Porcelain Company
475 Park Avenue
New York, New York 10022
(212) 838-7744

Crate & Barrel
(800) 323-5461
www.crateandbarrel.com

DK Schulman
(personalized invitations)
(860) 868-4300

Hermès
www.Hermes.com

Hollyhock
817 Hilldale Avenue
West Hollywood, California 90069
(310) 777-0100
www.hollyhockinc.com

Indigo Seas
123 North Robertson Boulevard
Los Angeles, California 90048
(310) 550-8758

Jeffrey Tillou Antiques
39 West Street
Litchfield, Connecticut 06759
(860) 567-9663
www.tillouantiques.com

Lacanche
(stoves and kitchen accessories)
www.lacanche.com

Liz O'Brien
800A Fifth Avenue
New York, New York 10021
(212) 755-3800
info@Lizobrien.com

Marshalls
www.MarshallsOnline.com

Mecox Gardens
962 Lexington Avenue
New York, New York 10021
(212) 249-5301
www.mecoxgardens.com

Michael Trapp, Inc.
7 River Road
West Cornwall, Connecticut 06796
(860) 672-6098
www.michaeltrapp.com

Munder Skiles
(garden furniture)
872 Madison Avenue
New York, New York 10021
(212) 717-0150

Neo-studio
25 Madison Street
Sag Harbor, New York 11963
(631) 725-6478
neo-studio@earthlink.net4

Nina Griscom
958 Lexington Avenue
New York, New York 10021
(212) 717-7373
info@ninagriscom.com

Personal Best
(monograms)
(860) 868-9966

D. Porthault at Bergdorf Goodman
754 Fifth Avenue
New York, New York 10019
(800) 558-1855

Pottery Barn
(888) 794-4044
www.potterybarn.com

Restoration Hardware
(800) 762-1005
www.restorationhardware.com

R. T. Facts Antiques
22 South Main Street
Kent, Connecticut 06757
(860) 927-1700
www.rtfacts.com

Gary Sergeant Antiques
88 Main Street North
Woodbury, Connecticut 06798
(203) 266-4177
www.gsergeant.com

Source Perrier
(888) 543-2804
www.sourceperrier.com

Sur la Table
(800) 243-0852
www.SurLaTable.com

TJ Maxx
www.TJMaxx.com

Target
www.target.com

Trianon Antiques
1845 North Main Street (Route 7)
Sheffield, Massachusetts 01257
(413) 528-0775

Vivre
www.Vivre.com

Waterworks
29 Park Avenue
Danbury, Connecticut 06810
(203) 792-8343
www.waterworks.com

White Flower Farm
(plants and natural meat)
P.O. Box 50 (Route 63)
Litchfield, Connecticut 06759
(800) 503-9624
www.whiteflowerfarm.com

William Sonoma
(888) 922-4110
www.williamsonoma.com

Wisteria
(800) 320-9757
www.wisteria

Yves Delorme
(sheets and towels)
www.yvesdelorme.com

Carpets

Doris Leslie Blau
306 East 61st Street
New York, New York 10021
(212) 586-5511
www.dorisleslieblau.com

Hockanson
D & D Building
979 Third Avenue, Suite 909
New York, New York 10022
(212) 758-0669

Stark
D & D Building
979 Third Avenue
New York, New York 10022
(212) 752-9000
www.starkcarpet.com

Fabric and Wallpaper

Brunschwig & Fils
75 Virginia Road
North White Plains, New York 10603
(914) 684-5800
staff@brunschwig.com

Christopher Hyland
D & D Building
979 Third Avenue, Suite 1710
New York, New York 10022
(212) 688-6121
info@christopherhyland.com

Clarence House
D & D Building
979 Third Avenue
New York, New York 10022
(212) 752-2890
www.clarencehouse.com

Payne
(to the trade)
(800) 543-4322

Pierre Deux
D & D Building
979 Third Avenue
New York, New York 10022
(212) 521-8012
www.pierredeux.com

Quadrille
D & D Building
979 Third Avenue
New York, New York 10022
(212) 753-2995

Auction Houses

Christie's
20 Rockefeller Plaza
New York, New York 10020
(212) 636-2000

Doyle New York
175 East 87th Street
New York, New York 10128
(212) 427-2730
info@DoyleNewYork.com

iGavel Inc.
229 East 120th Street
New York, New York 10035
(212) 289-5588
info@igavel.com

Litchfield County Auctions
425 Bantam Road (Route 202)
Litchfield, Connecticut 06759
(860) 567-4661; (212) 724-0156
info@lcainc.us
litchfieldcountyauctions.com

Rago Arts and Auction Center
(609) 397-9374

Sotheby's
1334 York Avenue
New York, New York 10021
(212) 606-7000

Specialty Foods and Kitchen Accessories

Eli Zabar
1411 Third Avenue
New York, New York 10028
(212) 717-8100
www.elizabar.com

Jacques Torres
285 Amsterdam Avenue
New York, New York 10023
(212) 787-3256

La Maison du Chocolat
1018 Madison Avenue
New York, New York 10021
(212) 744-7117
contact@lamaisonduchocolat.fr

Payard
(chocolate mendiants)
1032 Lexington Avenue
New York, New York 10021
(212) 717-5252
www.payard.com

The Pantry
5 Titus Road
Washington Depot, Connecticut 06794
(860) 868-0258

France

Baccarat
(tabletop and furnishings)
11 Place des Etats-Unis
75116 Paris
+33 (0) 1 40 22 11 00
www.baccarat.com

Blanc d'Ivoire
(accessories)
104 rue du Bac
75007 Paris
+33 (0) 1 45 44 41 17

Comptoir de Famille
(furniture and decorative objects)
34 rue Saint Sulpice
75006 Paris
+33 (0) 1 43 26 22 29
www.comptoirdefamille.com

Deyrolle
(taxidermy)
46 rue du Bac
75007 Paris
+33 (0) 1 42 22 30 07
www.deyrolle.com

Dîners en Ville
(tabletop)
27 rue de Varenne
75007 Paris
+33 (0) 1 42 22 78 33

Flamant
(furnishings and decorative objects)
8 rue de l'Abbaye
75006 Paris
+33 (0) 1 56 81 12 40

Habitat
+33 (0) 1 58 05 10 87
www.habitat.net

Hermès
(tabletop)
24 rue du Faubourg Saint Honoré
75008 Paris
+33 (0) 1 40 17 47 17

L'Artisan parfumeur
(perfume and room spray)
www.artisanparfumeur.com

Le Bon Marché
(tabletop)
22 rue de Sèvres
75007 Paris
+33 (0) 1 44 39 80 50;
+33 (0) 1 44 39 80 00

Le Cêdre Rouge
(decorative objects)
22 avenue Victoire
75001 Paris
+33 (0) 1 42 33 71 05

Le Grand Comptoir
(decorative objects)
116 rue du Bac
75007 Paris
+33 (0) 1 40 49 00 95

Marie Papier
(stationery and invitations)
26 rue Vavin
75006 Paris
+33 (0) 1 43 26 46 44

Maison du Monde
(decorative objects)
Forum des Halles, niveau 2
208 Porte Berger
75001 Paris
+33 (0) 2 53 40 83 01
www.maisonsdumonde.com

Mis en Demeure
(accessories)
27 rue du Cherche Midi
75006 Paris
+33 (0) 1 45 48 83 79

Pierre Frey
(fabrics and decorative objects)
+33 (0) 1 44 77 36 00

D. Porthault
(sheets, towels, and linen)
50 avenue Montaigne
75008 Paris
+33 (0) 1 47 20 75 25

Puyforcat
(silverware)
+33 (0) 1 44 77 53 77;
+33 (0) 1 45 63 10 10

Yves Delorme
(sheets, towels, and linen)
+33 (0) 4 77 23 67 67

Antiques and Accessories

Ader Societé de ventes Volontaires
8 rue Saint Marc
75002 Paris
+33 (0) 1 53 40 77 10
www.ader-paris.fr

Alexandre Biaggi
(twentieth-century art and decoration, Art
Deco, *curiositiés*)
14 rue de Seine
75006 Paris
+33 (0) 1 44 07 34 73

Anne Sophie Duval
(twentieth-century furniture, Art Deco,
curiositiés)
5 quai Malaquais
75006 Paris
+33 (0) 1 43 54 51 16

Au Vieux Paris
(*orfevrerie*)
4 rue de la Paix
75002 Paris
+33 (0) 1 42 61 00 89

Didier Aaron
(eighteenth- and nineteenth-century
furniture and decorative objects)
118 rue du Faubourg Saint Honoré
75008 Paris
+33 (0) 1 47 42 47 34

Galerie Camoin-Demachy
(eighteenth-, nineteenth-, and twentieth-
century furniture, Art Deco, carpets,
curiosités)
9 quai Voltaire
75007 Paris
+33 (0) 1 42 61 82 06

Galerie Perpitch
(sixteenth- and seventeenth-century
furniture, *curiosités*)
240 boulevard Saint Germain
75007 Paris
+33 (0) 1 45 48 37 67

Galerie Ratton-Ladriere
(sculpture of the middle ages, *curiosités*,
paintings)
11 quai Voltaire
75007 Paris
+33 (0) 1 42 61 29 79

Maroum H. Saloum
(decorative objects, Art Deco, *curiosités*,
eighteenth-, nineteenth-, and twentieth-
century furniture)
6 rue de Lille
75007 Paris
+33 (0) 1 40 15 95 01

Philippe Vichot
(eighteenth- and nineteenth-century
furniture, *curiosités*)
37 rue de Lille
75007 Paris
+33 (0) 1 40 15 00 81

Vallois
(twentieth-century furniture, Art Deco)
41 rue de Seine
75006 Paris
+33 (0) 1 43 29 50 84

Specialty Foods and Kitchen Accessories

Fauchon
(specialty foods)
24-26 Place de la Madeleine
75008 Paris
+33 (0) 1 70 39 38 00
www.fauchon.com

Fouquet
(chocolates, caramel, teas, spices)
22 rue François 1er
75008 Paris
+33 (0) 1 47 23 30 36
www.fouquet.fr

Hediard
(jams and pate de fruits)
2 place de la Madeleine
75008 Paris
+33 (0) 1 43 12 88 88
www.hediard.com

Ladurée
(chocolates, macarons, and cakes)
21 rue Bonaparte
75006 Paris
+33 (0) 1 44 07 64 87
16 rue Royale
+33 (0) 1 42 60 21 79
75008 Paris
www.laduree.com